Praise for *The Go-Giver Marriage*

"Falling in love is easy. Staying in love? That's the tricky part. John and Ana have written a beautiful tribute to the joys and challenges of marriage, followed by actionable steps to keep the relationship strong. This is a book that couples will come back to again and again."

—HARVILLE HENDRIX, PhD & HELEN LAKELLY HUNT, PhD, coauthors of the
New York Times bestseller *Getting the Love You Want: A Guide for Couples*

"This sweet, simple story conveys the essence of true love—and the simple daily practices that keep that love alive. *The Go-Giver Marriage* is a gem, destined to be a classic that couples will read for generations."

—DAVID BACH, 10X *New York Times* bestselling author of *Smart Women Finish Rich* and *The Automatic Millionaire*

"Written from honest experience and with immense compassion, Ana and John's book gives an actionable roadmap toward real lasting love in any relationship."

—MARIE FORLEO, author of the #1 *New York Times* bestseller *Everything Is Figureoutable*

"All the charm, wit, and insight of the original classic. *The Go-Giver* helped hundreds of thousands of people find more relevance, fulfillment, and success in their business lives. We predict *The Go-Giver Marriage* will do the same for their relationships."

—JON & KATHRYN GORDON, bestselling authors of *Relationship Grit*

"This delightful book offers a blueprint for creating—and sustaining—a loving marriage. *The Go-Giver Marriage* is a must-read for all couples seeking to keep their love alive and flourishing."

—SUSAN WINTER, bestselling author of *Older Women/Younger Men* and relationship expert (*Oprah, The Today Show, GMA*, et al.)

"*The Go-Giver Marriage* is for everyone who is married, might get married, or just wants richer relationships. The story gets into your head and sinks into your heart—and then it changes you. I believe it will make a powerful difference in your life."

—DAN ROCKWELL, creator of the *Leadership Freak* blog

"A delightful story filled with practical wisdom for a happier and more loving marriage. We highly recommend it!"

—RORY VADEN, *New York Times* bestselling author of *Take the Stairs* and AJ VADEN, cofounder and CEO of Brand Builders Group

"*The Go-Giver Marriage* is a beautiful book, filled with practical, caring ways to give your best self to the one you love. I wholeheartedly believe it will enrich every life—and every relationship—it touches."

—KEN BLANCHARD, coauthor of *The One Minute Manager*® and *Leading at a Higher Level*

"Full of inspiration and wisdom, the entertaining stories in *The Go-Giver Marriage* make the true, time-tested secrets of a happy marriage jump off the pages and into your heart."

—LAURA DOYLE, *New York Times* bestselling author, international relationship expert, and host of *The Empowered Wife* podcast

"One firefly can distinguish itself only by becoming a blazing beacon of incandescent brilliance. There are many marriage books but this book is that firefly. It's for everyone, married or not-yet, who desires the ultimate in joy from living with another person. Truly life-changing."

—RABBI DANIEL LAPIN, President of the American Alliance of Jews and Christians, radio and TV host

"*The Go-Giver Marriage* is a beautiful treasure map—not just for happy, intentional partnerships but also for happy, intentional humans. Whether you're coupled, uncoupled, or seeking your soul mate, this is a must-read if you want to find deep answers to key questions you never thought to ask."

—CHRISTINE KANE, author of *The Soul-Sourced*™ *Entrepreneur*, founder and CEO of Uplevel You

"A beautiful story, both entertaining and wise—and its message is exactly what millions of couples need right now. Many marriages will be helped, perhaps even saved, by this little book."

—GEORGE PRATT, PhD, Vice-Chairman of Psychology at Scripps Memorial Hospital, La Jolla, California

"So many sweet, profound surprises in this book—it's like unwrapping a beautiful gift. I didn't want this story to end. I may read it 100 times."

—DONDI SCUMACI, author of *Designed for Success: The 10 Commandments for Women in the Workplace*

"*The Go-Giver Marriage* is a powerful story that will benefit your marriage at any stage. Read it, take it to heart—and unleash the full potential of lasting love."

—SKIP PRICHARD, President & CEO of OCLC, Inc., bestselling author of *The Book of Mistakes: 9 Secrets to Creating a Successful Future*

"I loved the sweet and meaningful journey with its simple, practical lessons. Reminiscent of *The 5 Love Languages*, but unique and rich with symbolism. The fable-within-a-fable story of the young lovers and the tree reads like a love song for all couples."

—ABBIE MCCLUNG, MBA, Communications Manager, Klamath Basin Behavioral Health, Oregon

"What a book, what a message—love, appreciation, and the spirit of generosity. The world is long overdue for the 5 secrets to lasting love!"

—MICHAEL J. MAHER, bestselling author of (7L) *The Seven Levels of Communication* and coauthor of *The Miracle Morning for REA*

"In creating wedding and anniversary events for hundreds of couples, I have seen firsthand the qualities that lead to long-lasting marriages. *The Go-Giver Marriage* gets to the heart of what creates the kind of magic we all want in our relationships. It will also make an ideal wedding or engagement gift!"

—COLIN COWIE, Colin Cowie Lifestyle

"*The Go-Giver Marriage* taps into the essence of what truly counts, not just in a marriage but in *any* relationship, and weaves that into a story that makes it unforgettable and immediately applicable. We cannot wait to share it with others!"

—TARA ELLIS-ROGERS, Managing Partner, Mojo PR, Dubai

"An engaging and inspiring fable that guides readers through the essentials of a positively transformative relationship. For these two coauthors, 'stratospheric happiness' is no fiction!"

—DAVID KRUEGER, MD, "Best Doctors in America" (Woodward/White), 2021
Executive Mentor Coach of the Year (International Association of Top Professionals)

"What a powerful and enlightening book this is! Ana and John thoughtfully and creatively show us how living life bountifully is a blessing—for ourselves and for those we love."

—NIDO R. QUBEIN, President, High Point University

"As I read, I found myself thinking, 'I *know* this'—but then asking, 'Yeah . . . but do I *do* this?' What a great, wonderfully *useful* book. I love it. We *both* love it!"

—GARY BURR, Nashville Hall of Fame hit songwriter and cofounder (with
his wife, Georgia Middleman, and Kenny Loggins) of Blue Sky Riders

"Succinct, wise, insightful, and above all, immensely practical. Let this quick read shine a light on your marriage—and then take it to the next level and see just how fulfilling life can be!"

—JOSEPHINE M. GROSS, PhD, Editor in Chief of *Networking
Times*, cofounder of Gabriel Media Group, Inc.

The Go-Giver
Marriage

The Go-Giver Marriage

A Little Story About
the 5 Secrets to Lasting Love

John David Mann
Ana Gabriel Mann, MA

BenBella Books, Inc.

Dallas, TX

BenBella Books, Inc.
10440 N. Central Expressway
Suite 800
Dallas, TX 75231
benbellabooks.com
Send feedback to feedback@benbellabooks.com

BenBella is a federally registered trademark.

Printed in the United States of America
10 9 8 7 6 5 4 3 2 1

Library of Congress Control Number: 2021040504
ISBN 9781637740811
eISBN 9781637740828

Editing by Gregory Brown
Copyediting by Jennifer Brett Greenstein
Proofreading by Lisa Story and Cape Cod Compositors, Inc.
Text design and composition by Aaron Edmiston
Cover design by Joe Montgomery
Jacket photograph © Angelo Hornak/Getty
Printed by Lake Book Manufacturing

To Alfred and Carolyn Mann, Roger and Sylvia Burt, and Mike and Myrna Burg, who showed us what lasting love looks like.

And to Sarah, Michelle, Nick, Chris, and Kaia: thank you for being our teachers—we love you dearly!

Contents

The Parable

1. Tom

The first thing Tom noticed as he stepped inside the office was how elevated it felt, as if he were standing in an eagle's nest high up on some craggy cliff.

Maybe it was the floor-to-ceiling windows, or the sparse furnishings. No big executive desk. No plush chairs. Just a few high-tech saddle-top rolling stools and, off to one corner, an adjustable standing desk, like an architect's drafting table. A series of framed black-and-white photos dotted the walls. Nothing distracted from the spectacular view of the distant western mountains, half shrouded in slate-gray clouds.

If the next two hours went well, soon this could be *his* office.

"So, the big day arrives."

The man perched at the desk was so still, Tom had practically forgotten he was there.

With his sleepy brown eyes, bushy eyebrows, and still, wise face, he looked like an owl.

"Yessir, Mr. Janell," said Tom.

"Jeremiah will do." The man nodded toward the stool nearest to Tom.

"Yessir." Tom took his seat, sure his heartbeat must be audible clear across the room.

"Nervous?" Jeremiah didn't look up from the sheet of paper he was reviewing, no doubt a summary of Tom's personnel file.

Tom hesitated.

"No need," said the man. "This won't hurt a bit."

Tom started to chuckle but stopped when he realized the other man had not smiled. Surely it was a joke, though, right?

"Nossir," he said.

Tom was face-to-face with the chief operating officer—soon to retire—of Rachel's Famous Coffee. It was the second most important post, after CEO, in a massive global enterprise, a coveted position for which there was intense competition.

The very position for which Tom was interviewing.

He had already been through a series of preliminary sessions, including two with the board of directors. Reams of questions had been asked and answered, his work history examined, higher-ups' opinions formed and shared behind closed doors. The only hurdles left were his next meeting an hour from now with the CEO—and this one.

Who, me, nervous?

"Do you mind if I take notes . . . sir?"

Despite its size, Rachel's Famous Coffee still had the feel of a small business—almost an *un*corporation. When you worked at Rachel's, you became family. Still, this was the COO. Tom couldn't quite bring himself to call the man by his first name.

Mr. Janell looked up and gave a slow blink, making the owl impression even more striking. "Of course," he said.

Tom pulled a notebook from an inside jacket pocket and set it open on one knee. He didn't actually expect to write much down;

Tom had an excellent memory. It was just that doodling helped put him at ease.

"You're young," the man murmured, his eyes back on the sheet of paper. "But your work is impressive."

"Thank you, sir." Tom knew this was true; he had a knack for team building. It was Tom who'd led the charge to open dozens of new stores in key locations and build out the Rachel's Famous Coffee brand on a national scale. He'd even designed the company's now-iconic *R* logo himself. A "rising star," they'd called him. Still, he also knew there were other equally qualified candidates. In the end, he suspected it really came down to his interviewer's gut sense. And though he knew the man from dozens of management meetings and company events, Jeremiah Janell was a quiet, private person, and Tom could hardly claim to know him well.

It was rumored that Jeremiah was friends with Pindar, the legendary consultant who'd helped found this company, which lent the COO an almost mythic status.

He also had a reputation for being a bit . . . unusual. Tom had heard one VP refer to Jeremiah affectionately as having "a touch of the eccentric."

"I should tell you," said the COO, his eyes still on that single page, "some of these questions may get personal. All right?"

"Absolutely," said Tom. He wiped his palms on his trouser legs.

"By the end of the day," the man added, "you'll be ready to let us know if you're the right person for the job."

"I'm looking forward to it, sir," said Tom.

Wait.

Had he just said, *"You'll* be ready to let *us* know?"

Had Tom heard that backward?

Jeremiah tucked the page into a folder and filed it away on an unseen shelf behind him, then focused his gaze on Tom.

"When you were young and people asked you what you wanted to be when you grew up, what did you say?"

"An astronaut," Tom replied. "And later, an aviator. For a while there I wanted to be an archaeologist." He grinned. "But only if I could wear a fedora and go on expeditions like Indiana Jones."

He thought that would get a laugh, loosen things up a bit.

The COO just gave another one of those slow, owlish blinks.

"What is your favorite book?"

"Lord of the Rings would be in my top three," Tom replied. "Along with *The Alchemist*. But if I were stranded on a desert island and had to choose just one? That would have to be *The Little Prince.*"

"Oh? And what," said Jeremiah, "do you love about those three in particular?"

"Well," said Tom. "They're all adventure stories."

Jeremiah stared at him as if to say, *And?*

"Adventure stories . . . with a meaning, I guess you'd say," Tom added.

"Adventure stories . . . with a meaning," echoed Jeremiah.

Why had he repeated Tom's answer? Was that good? Or bad? Was Tom trying too hard to read the man's reactions?

He wiped his palms on his pant legs again.

"Question three: Who are your heroes? Alive or dead, doesn't matter."

"Honestly, and I don't mean this to sound ingratiating, but I think my number one hero is Rachel." Tom nodded at the series of black-and-whites on the wall. The photos were all shots of children's faces, mostly taken in village settings, and all by Rachel herself. Breathtakingly beautiful. Tom was well familiar with these portraits because they, or others like them, graced the walls everywhere in their corporate offices and in thousands of Rachel's Famous Coffee shops around the world, offering glimpses into the lives of their coffee-growing partners around the planet—communities that Rachel's had helped survive and thrive. "I've always been inspired by how this company has had such a positive impact on so many people's lives around the world."

It was a corporate story Tom had told and retold a thousand times over the past ten years.

"Next question," said Jeremiah. "You are seventy years old, still in robust health, your finances well in hand. You've retired from your career. No other obligations. You have unfettered time and the means to use it. What do you do?"

Tom hesitated again. He felt he ought to say something noble and philanthropic—volunteer his time for a charity, maybe. But he had no talent for bluffing or deceit.

"If I had no other responsibilities? I guess . . . I'd probably stay at home and write stories. Illustrated books, maybe."

"Like *The Little Prince*," said Jeremiah.

"Yes. Exactly."

Jeremiah nodded at Tom's little notebook and scooted his own stool a few feet closer. "May I see?"

Tom panicked. He had not planned to actually show his doodles to anyone—least of all the man conducting the interview! But he couldn't exactly refuse, could he?

"Of . . . of course." He held out the open notebook, praying that Jeremiah would not be offended by what he'd drawn and end the interview then and there.

On the page was a sketch of an owl, perched on a high branch, staring down at a flying mouse who wore a cape and sat astride a large jet-powered coffee bean. It was ridiculously fanciful—but Tom never knew quite what his sketching hand would do.

Jeremiah blinked once. "It's very good."

"Thank you," Tom murmured, furiously willing himself not to blush.

Jeremiah rolled his stool back to his desk, steepled his fingers, and stared at Tom.

"So. You'd like to be chief operating officer of Rachel's Famous Coffee."

"I would, sir. Very much so."

"Really," said Jeremiah. "Why?"

Okay, thought Tom. *This is where the real interview starts.*

Why did he want this job? That was easy. For Jamie.

And for Tess.

He remembered the day they met. The *moment* they met. How could he ever forget?

She wore hiking boots, khaki shorts, a blouse of the most brilliant cornflower blue, her sandy hair haloed by the intense Ecuadorian sun.

"You must be Tom," she'd said. He could still recall the thrill that went up his spine hearing that voice breathe his name. Could you fall in love after hearing someone speak just four words? It was not a question he'd ever thought to ask, but now he knew the answer.

The two talked all day and into the night. She laughed at all his jokes, even the lame ones. She could carry on a conversation about anything. She wasn't just lovely—she was dazzling.

From that day on, they were inseparable.

Tom and Tess were both working as field scouts, traveling to markets around the globe to foster partnerships with their coffee suppliers. Exciting times, all that travel, all those places, cultures, people. The two had actually met many of the children in those black-and-white photos. Soon people in the company stopped referring to them as "Tess" and "Tom." Instead, they became "Tessandtom."

Those first few years were magical. They both adored working at Rachel's. They adored each other. Life was good.

And then Jamie was born and their world turned upside down.

Jamie's birth and infancy were fraught with problems. Some of the specialists they consulted declared his challenges "intractable," which Tess had refused to accept. One neurologist had sat them down and said, "My advice? Lower your expectations, go home, and have another."

Tom had wanted to sue the guy. Tess had wanted to murder him.

Finding and securing all the different therapies Jamie needed took an enormous amount of time and energy. Money, which had never been much of an issue, was suddenly a very big issue indeed. Within a few very long years, they were financially and emotionally exhausted.

The honeymoon, glorious as it had been, was over.

Jeremiah was patiently waiting for an answer to his question.

COO was a position of enormous responsibility and would come with a huge bump in pay, something they sorely needed after the last six hellish years.

Unlike his current post as national field director, it was also very much a home-office position. If he got this promotion, Tom would no longer be constantly flying around the country. Reading his son bedtime stories would become more than a once-in-a-while thing.

"I love everything about Rachel's," said Tom. "Have loved every post I've held here over the past ten years. Right now, though, a position that keeps me home more would be a good thing for my family."

Jeremiah gave a slow blink. "Tess," he said, nodding. "We've missed her."

"Smartest person I know," said Tom.

"And your boy, he must be . . . five?"

"Just turned six." Tom paused. "Jamie has special needs."

Special needs.

Talk about a euphemism. Two bland words that barely scratched the surface. How about *heart-wrenching* needs? Or *overwhelming* needs?

"I remember," murmured Jeremiah. "It all must have been quite stressful."

Stressful. Another bland word. Try *nightmarish. Soul-crushing. Emotionally and financially cataclysmic.*

Tom nodded slowly. "Yessir, yes it has been. There were some rough years there. But we survived." He took a breath—and then astonished himself by blurting out, "And, hey, we still totally love each other, and that's the bottom line, right?"

He immediately regretted the words. That was *way* too personal. He felt as if he'd just veered his car off the road and straight into a ditch.

Jeremiah gave him a long, thoughtful look. Frowned. And then slowly shook his head.

"No," he said. "Not really."

Tom opened his mouth, then abruptly closed it.

Wait—*what?*

For the first time since their interview began, Jeremiah unfolded his long legs and rose to his feet. In his vest and shirtsleeves, slim tailored pants, and classic two-tone wingtips, he struck Tom as a figure from another era. Silently, he stalked along the far side of the office until he stopped at one particular photo on the adjacent wall.

This one was different from the others: a long shot of a snowcapped mountain, a tiny group of climbers huddled on its summit.

Jeremiah gazed at the photo, then turned again to Tom.

"To say love is what makes a marriage work is like saying it takes oxygen to climb a mountain. Yes, oxygen is necessary. But not sufficient."

Tom stared at the man. All he could think of was what that VP had said. *A touch of the eccentric.*

"They say 'love conquers all,'" Jeremiah continued, "but this cannot be true. There is too much evidence to the contrary. Look around you. You see people who end up hurting the ones they love. Who, in one way or another, love each other unhappily. Whose love turns to contempt or, worse, indifference. Whose love doesn't *last*.

"No, Tom, simply *being* in love cannot itself be the secret to a lasting, happy marriage."

Tom gave the only reply he could come up with. "Then what is?"

"Giving," said Jeremiah at once.

"Giving?"

"Giving."

How had this interview turned so weird so fast?

"Um . . . giving what?"

"Giving gifts, Tom," said Jeremiah, as if it were the most obvious thing in the world. He turned back to gaze again at the mountaintop photo. "I don't mean trinkets or toys," he added. "I mean genuine gifts."

Tom's mind raced.

Exactly what test or interview tactic was happening here?

And then, with one question, Jeremiah sent Tom's thoughts hurtling off a cliff of confusion.

"Tell me, Tom," the owl-man said. "What is the purpose of marriage?"

2. Tess

Tess sat in her parked car out behind the school and burst into tears.

It was the phone call from Amy that broke the dam.

The day had not started out well. Jamie was digging in his heels that morning. Getting him ready had been like wrestling an octopus. Tom was no help at all, and Tess had gotten so irritated she'd barked at him—which she now felt terrible about.

She'd known how nervous Tom was. This was, after all, the Big Day. He'd been all *no-sweat-I-got-this* for the past twenty-four hours, but she knew that was only bravado.

By the time she had Jamie ready to load into the car, Tom had already left. Had she wished him good luck? She couldn't honestly be sure. She'd meant to.

Then there'd been that video conference disaster. Ten minutes in and her cell phone buzzed: trouble at school. Jamie was in the school nurse's office crying. Apologizing all over herself, Tess had cut the video conference short. For the third time.

"That's the end of that client," she muttered to herself. And a hefty consulting fee they couldn't afford to lose.

Then, school.

Poor Jamie had had an accident in the classroom. A few kids—the usual suspects—made fun of him until he cried, which only made the teasing escalate. By the time the school nurse called Tess from her office, Jamie was inconsolable. It took Tess nearly forty minutes to get him settled, buoyed, and ready to reenter the classroom.

After that, she'd retreated to her car, where she sat, feeling that knot in the pit of her stomach, unsure whether she was about to burst into tears or scream in frustration.

And then she'd gotten the phone call. Amy, her best friend, was—

Tap-tap-tap.

The sound made Tess jump. It was Mrs. Delaney, the remedial reading teacher, knocking on Tess's car window.

Sorry! the woman mouthed soundlessly.

Tess put up one finger—*Hang on a sec!*—as she started the car so she could buzz down the window.

"Are you all right, dear?" the woman said.

Dee Delaney was Jamie's favorite teacher. She was kind to Jamie; more than that, she genuinely enjoyed him. She *got* Jamie, and he knew it. He might be learning-disabled and processing-disordered—"slow," as the other parents so condescendingly put it—but Jamie knew all about cruelty and kindness. He knew more about both of those than most kids ever would. "He's a wise little soul," Dee had observed the first day she met the boy.

"I'm fine," said Tess. "Rough morning."

"I heard what happened. I'm so sorry. They can be so mean. And he's such a sweetheart."

That he was. Tess would never forget the day he was born, the feeling of sitting up in bed and staring at him in her arms, marveling over how she had fallen so totally in love with this little lump of deliciousness. Wondering how anything could be so perfect. Tess ranked the day of Jamie's birth as Best Day Ever.

Made her heart ache to think about it.

"You sure you're all right?" said Dee.

"My husband's having a big interview today. We all feel the pressure. And I think I just lost a client." Tess took a big breath, then blew it out. "I'm fine," she repeated. "But thank you."

Mrs. Delaney nodded dubiously. She walked around to the driver's side of her own car, climbed in, and started the engine. Then she buzzed down her front passenger seat window and smiled over at Tess. "Your husband works at Rachel's Famous Coffee?" she said through the two open car windows.

"National field director. Up for chief operations officer."

"Didn't you used to work there as well?"

Tess nodded. "It's where we met."

Actually, that was another candidate for Best Day Ever: the day this gangly young field rep showed up at their base camp in Ecuador, all awkward and sweet and blushing. The memory of him staring at her never failed to make Tess smile. He'd made a lame joke, and she'd surprised herself by laughing, charmed by his earnestness. She laughed all that day and all through the evening. At some point she persuaded him to show her his sketchbook. He began narrating each drawing as if it were a scene in a movie, and she would laugh and say, "Tell me more."

A year later they were married—and a year after that she was sitting up in bed with this tiny little marvel looking back at her.

The day of Jamie's birth also proved pivotal in more ways than one. At six days, Tess and Tom were both still giddy with that mix of bliss and exhaustion typical of new parents everywhere.

At six weeks, it was clear there were problems.

At six months, they faced reality. The extended maternity leave Tess had taken wasn't going to be temporary after all. Tess wasn't going back to her job in another month, or another two months. She wasn't going back at all.

Leaving Rachel's was a wrenching decision. Tess was a talented strategist, with an intuitive ability to grasp the complexities of a situation and restructure logistics on the fly. She was outstanding at the job, and she loved it. But once they saw just how challenged Jamie was, she knew she had no choice. Assessing and solving complex problems—this was what she did best. It was what had made her so valuable at work. Now she needed to apply those skills to supporting their child.

Still, that day? The day they acknowledged the truth of their situation and made that decision?

Worst Day Ever.

"You think he'll be okay today?" Dee was saying. "Your husband, I mean."

Tess paused before answering. "I do," she said. "They'd be crazy not to give it to him."

"But you're nervous for him."

"A wreck."

She took another big breath and glanced over at Dee, who sat, not saying a word. No wonder she was such a great teacher. She was an excellent listener.

"I'm a little shook up," said Tess. "I got a call just now, from an old friend."

She and Amy went to school together, got married the same year, same month. Now Amy and Alex were going through an "amicable divorce," whatever that was supposed to mean. When Amy told her, Tess felt like she'd been poleaxed. "Oh, Amy . . . what happened?" she'd said. "You guys were *crazy* about each other!" But Amy didn't really have an answer. No big fights. Nobody cheated. They just . . . well, Amy didn't exactly know what happened. Their marriage just sort of seemed to slip away.

"I don't know why it upset me so much," Tess added after describing the call to Dee.

After all, that would never happen to her and Tom. They were every bit as in love with each other now as they'd been that long-ago day in Ecuador, right? And it wasn't as if they were fighting or arguing or anything.

So why that gigantic knot in the pit of her stomach?

"Marriage can be quite the puzzle," said Dee.

"I guess," Tess murmured. She looked over at Dee through the two open car windows and gave a rueful smile. "I suppose we could be having this conversation in the same car."

Dee frowned, then said, "I've got a better idea. Do you have a little time free right now?" She patted her empty front passenger's seat. "There's someone I'd love to have you meet. I was just on my way over there."

Tess hesitated.

She wasn't due to pick Jamie up for speech therapy for another two hours, so, in theory, she should have time. But there were no guarantees she wouldn't get another call from the school an hour from now. Or ten minutes from now.

"If you have to cut it short," Dee added, "it's not a problem. It's not far, and I can drive you back at a moment's notice." She smiled. "Maybe we'll untangle that puzzle."

Tess debated for another few seconds, then shut off the engine and hopped out.

"Why not?" She put on a smile she wasn't sure she felt.

Right now, she thought, *I'd be happy if I could just untangle that knot in my stomach.*

3. The Tree

What is the purpose of marriage?

The question hung in the air between them.

"The purpose of marriage?" repeated Tom. "Wow." He'd never really thought about that. Companionship? Security? Affection? He thought some more. "Having someone on your side, I guess? Someone to share your burdens and responsibilities?"

Jeremiah blinked slowly. "All right. But what's the *purpose*?"

"For Tess and me, I guess I'd say it's to create a good home for our son. To make sure he has the best possible start in life."

"Children grow and leave, Tom. Then what?"

Tom was bewildered. Where was this all going?

"You love each other," said Jeremiah. "You have kids. You live, you age. You have good times and hard times. What's the point?"

The point?

The man took one more look at the mountaintop scene in the photo on the wall and then stepped back across the room to retake his saddle-top perch.

"Let me tell you a story," he said.

"Once there was a young man who fell in love with a very beautiful princess. From summer to fall to winter to spring he wooed her, and on the first of June the two were married. 'From today,' the young man declared, 'June the first will forever be the happiest day of the year.'"

Okay, thought Tom, *now* this *is the weirdest job interview I've ever had.*

"After the wedding," Jeremiah continued, "they moved into a little cottage together . . ."

Every day the young man went off to work, building roads and bridges. And every day the princess went to work herself, out in the backyard if the weather was good, or inside when it rained, setting up her easel in the living room, where she painted night scenes: starry skies, dark silhouettes of trees against the purple clouds.

People bought her paintings and hung them in their homes, and between the income from her art and the young man's construction pay, they lived a modest but comfortable life.

Every afternoon the young man came home and said, "I love you!" and the princess said, "I love you too!" and then they sat down to a simple dinner together.

One day, coming home from work, the young man was surprised to see a little sapling growing in the midst of their front yard. He didn't know how it got there. He hadn't planted it. It was just there.

Every day, the little sapling grew larger. Within a few months it was a sturdy, elegant little tree with bright green leaves rustling and whispering in the breeze.

Some days, the leaves rustled and whispered even when the young man couldn't feel any breeze at all.

He could not quite tell what the whispers were saying, but he thought it was the most beautiful sound in the world.

On the hottest days of summer, the little tree provided enough shade to keep their cottage cool. During rainstorms it protected them from the wind. Sometimes they would go out during the cool of the evening and sit under its branches, resting against the trunk, and read to each other.

One morning on his way to work, the young man noticed a row of buds jutting out of one branch. When he returned late that afternoon, the branch bore a dozen flowers. He stepped closer and was startled to see that they were bright blood-red roses.

Roses, on a tree?

Amazing!

The fall soon arrived, with winter nipping at its heels. Frosts settled over the fields and everywhere throughout the kingdom flora and fauna withdrew for a long winter's sleep.

But the little tree continued to flourish, its leaves and flowers as full and lively as ever.

Roses, on a tree, in the winter!

Soon the spring storms were upon them. Some nights the wind blew hard and ferocious rains pummeled the kingdom, driving farmers to cover their crops and orchards for fear of terrible damage.

But the little tree was unharmed.

By May the weather was beautiful again.

Then one late-May morning the young man came upon something disturbing in the path: a little cluster of dead, dried-up rose petals. He looked up in alarm at the little tree's branches. They had begun to droop.

He told his wife, "It's just the seasons. All plants do this."

"In May?" she said.

"It's a phase," he said. "It's just finding its own cycle."

But they both knew this wasn't true.

That night a warm breeze blew. He listened out the bedroom window for the whisper of the leaves, but the tree was silent.

Within a few days, all the flowers were gone.

Though the two young lovers did not speak of it, they both sensed something was wrong with their tree. But what? The weather was perfect. Other trees and plants around them were doing well.

But not this one.

June first arrived: their first wedding anniversary!

They both stopped work early that day and held a picnic under their little tree. The food was good, but their conversation was stilted. The listless little tree cast a gloomy shadow over the proceedings.

That evening, lugging their baskets and tablecloths back inside, the young man turned to his wife and told her that he loved her.

But instead of saying, "I love you too!" she looked at him and said, "You do?"

"Of course! More than anything in the world! More than there are stars in the sky!"

"Oh, good," said the princess. She thought for a moment, then said, "How, exactly?"

The young man put the basket down and stared at her. "What do you mean?"

"How," she repeated. "What is it you love about me?"

"Everything!" he said. "I love *everything* about you."

She frowned. "Yeah," she said. "But what *exactly*? I need specifics here."

"You're very beautiful," he said.

She shrugged. "Every woman is beautiful when she's young. What is it you love about me in particular?"

"Well," he said. "You're the most thoughtful person I've ever known."

"Really?"

The young man nodded.

"Wow," she said. "Thanks."

"You're welcome," he said. "It's true."

She smiled.

The next morning he kissed her goodbye, set off down the front path to work—and stopped in his tracks.

The tree stood tall, its leaves chattering and giggling in the June breeze.

Sprouting from the lowest branch were a dozen fresh new blood-red roses.

The room fell silent.

Tom was baffled. A princess. A tree that grew roses.

What on earth were they talking about?!

4. Nicole's Story

The two women pulled into a big circular drive and parked in front of a beautiful stone mansion. The moment Dee cut the engine, Tess heard a voice calling from behind the building.

"Out back!"

"Quite the place," Tess whispered as they followed a slate path around back.

"The professor is quite the character," Dee whispered back.

On the ride over, Tess had learned that Dee was part of a small group of women who called themselves the Marriage Project, and that they were all meeting at the home of someone Dee referred to as "the professor."

Judging from the size of the place, Tess thought the professing business must be doing awfully well.

The path opened onto a huge yard bordered by a broad slate terrace, where three women were setting out glass tumblers and a few pitchers of something that looked iced and delicious. Tess filed away their names as Dee made the introductions.

The professor, evidently, was yet to arrive.

"We were just talking about the puzzle of marriage," explained Dee. "So I kidnapped her."

"You've come to the right place!" said the first woman, Nicole, who had a smile that made Tess want to reach for her sunglasses. "That's what brought us all here!"

"The conundrum of matrimony," the second woman agreed. "Enigma of hitchedness." This one's name was Gillian.

The third woman, Melanie, gave Tess a quiet smile, then glanced over at Gillian, who said, "Right," and turned to Dee. "We're gonna go see what Sofia's cooking up, bring out some munchies."

Gillian and Melanie retreated into the building while Nicole took a seat next to Tess and began to tell her story.

Nicole Martin was a schoolteacher turned educational software entrepreneur. Ten years earlier, she had hit a crossroads: her business was booming, but her marriage was in trouble.

"No bitter arguments or anything like that," she clarified. "I could even say we were happy . . . more or less. But not truly, fully happy. Not *stratospherically* happy. There was something we'd had when we first got married that was getting lost along the way. It was like a nagging cough that doesn't seem that bad, but that you sense could turn into something worse."

Tess felt the knot in her stomach tighten. That sounded just like what Amy had said on the phone. *No big fights. Nobody cheated. The marriage just sort of seemed to slip away.*

"I knew Dee from school," Nicole continued, "and she suggested I go see the professor."

On Nicole's first visit, the professor asked her to describe three things she loved about her husband.

"I said, 'First off, he's a terrific guy—'

"'No, no, no!' the professor shouted. 'No generalizations! *Terrific* could mean anything—so it means nothing! No, no, no, no, *no*! Tell me something *real*. Something meaningful. Something specific!'"

Tess heard Dee chuckling at Nicole's impassioned professor impression.

Nicole continued. "Fine. So I thought for a moment . . . and I couldn't come up with anything! I was mortified. Finally, I blurted out, 'He makes a wicked lasagna.' Felt like an idiot saying it, too—but the professor sat there nodding and beaming, like I'd said something profound. 'Good, good! What else?'

"But that was it. Sitting there, in that moment, that was all I could think of. How pathetic is that?"

Nicole said the professor sent her home with a two-part assignment. First, starting with the "wicked lasagna," she was to build a list of five specific things she loved about her husband.

"And that was my initiation into the First Secret."

"First secret?" said Tess.

"Appreciation," said Nicole.

Dee leaned over. "The professor calls them the 5 Secrets to Lasting Love."

"Appreciation comes first," said Nicole, "because it's the foundation of all the others. And it's so basic—yet so many people do the opposite and keep a running list of things that bother them about the other person."

"Familiarity breeds contempt," commented Tess.

"Exactly! One of those handy little bits of 'folk wisdom' that people take as gospel truth. *No, no, no, no, no.*" She flashed that

27

dazzling smile. "As the professor would say. Familiarity does *not* breed contempt—or at least it doesn't have to. Because it's just as easy to go the other way, you know. To keep a running list of things you *love*.

"You can look for things to criticize or look for things to appreciate. They're equally easy. It's purely a question of where you put your focus. And what you focus on increases. All it takes is a decision, and it's a choice you make over and over."

"Hence the list," said Tess.

"And the next part of the homework," Dee added. "Actually telling him the five things on the list."

Nicole laughed. "Right. Which was a whole other revelation."

"Really," said Tess. "How so?"

"To me, that felt . . . weird. Awkward. Like working a set of muscles I hadn't used in ages. I sat him down and said, 'Honey, I've got some things I need to tell you.' And it just about knocked him over! We'd been married nearly seven years at that point, and I don't think I'd ever seen him so at a loss for words.

"Finally, he said, 'Wow.' And then, 'Thank you.' That was it. No big dramatic scene. We went on with our day. But something had shifted—something seismic.

"I kept doing the homework. A few months later, for our seventh anniversary, I gave him a little booklet I'd made up titled '100 Things I Love About You.'"

She flashed her dazzling smile once more.

"That was ten years ago. The list is still growing."

Tess frowned.

"What are you thinking?" said Dee softly.

"I don't know. That just seems . . ."

"A little simplistic?" said Dee.

"I suppose," Tess admitted. *Far-fetched* was the word she was thinking. "Honestly, I could name a dozen things I love about Tom right off the bat."

"Okay," said Nicole, in a tone that said, *Go on.*

Tess blinked. "What, right now?" She looked at Dee, then back at Nicole. "Okay, let's see . . ." She thought about Tom getting ready to leave that morning.

Tess had to admit, she was still irritated with him. She could see he was intimidated by some of the other job candidates, and terrified that he would blow the interview and come home empty-handed, which she understood. But couldn't he have taken even thirty seconds to help her get Jamie ready and out the door?

She realized that the others were looking at her.

"Right!" she said. "A dozen things." She frowned again. Then she thought back to the evening before, after dinner . . . and smiled.

"He loves to read to our son—he's a great storyteller. He's ambitious, which I love. He's a great kisser." She blushed. "That's three, right there."

"Excellent!" said Nicole. "Does he know you love all those things about him?"

"Of course he does."

"Really?" said Nicole.

"Well, yeah."

"How do you know he knows?"

"Because . . . he just *knows*."

And the moment she said it, she wondered if it was really true.

Nicole nodded sympathetically. "You have a son, you said?"

"Jamie. Just turned six."

"Then you already know this: How often do you need to tell Jamie how wonderful he is, how amazing, delicious, powerful, how *good* he is?"

"Every day," Tess replied immediately. "Multiple times a day."

"As often as possible, right?" said Nicole. "Because life is full of hard edges. It bruises you, wears you down. Being reminded how magnificent you are builds you back up again. Children need that. And no matter how grown-up and sophisticated we are, every one of us is still a child on the inside."

Tess flashed again on Tom reading to Jamie, the two of them laughing, and she realized that was one more thing she loved about him—those moments when she caught glimpses of the little boy inside.

Had she ever told him that?

"Let me ask you something," said Nicole. "Has your husband ever told you that you're beautiful?"

"All the time."

"Do you believe him?"

"No," Tess admitted, "I think he's delusional."

Nicole laughed. "Because love is . . ."

"Blind?"

"Exactly." She shook her head sadly. "Folk wisdom. It's the worst." She sighed. "And it isn't true, not at all. Love is not blind. Love has the eyes of an eagle."

Tess frowned again. She did not think of herself as beautiful.

"Let's say it this way," Nicole continued. "Every happily married man I've ever met swears he 'married up.' And typically his spouse says the exact same thing about him. Objectively speaking, how is that possible? How can they both claim the other is their 'better half' and mean it?"

"Because they're delusional?" said Tess.

She heard Dee chuckling again.

"Maybe," said Nicole. "Or maybe because they've both mastered the First Secret."

"Appreciating," said Tess.

"Appreciating."

"So . . . you're saying beauty is in the eye of the beholder."

"Not exactly," Nicole said gently. "Beauty is in the *beheld.* Because whether you know it or not, Tess, you really are that beautiful. It's just that he's taken the time and the care to see it."

Tess was silent.

"You know how every baby is cute?" Nicole continued. "How every puppy is adorable? With babies and puppies it's easy. Anyone can see it. Adults are more complicated, so for us it can take a little sharper vision."

"The eyes of an eagle," murmured Tess.

How often had Tom told her how beautiful she was? And how often had she brushed it off, dismissing him with a teasing "Only you would see it that way!" Well, what if he was the only one who'd really looked?

"Love doesn't blind, Tess," said Nicole. "It illuminates. And the more you practice looking for it, the more beauty and worthiness there is to see."

The three sipped their iced tea for a moment.

"I appreciate everything you're saying," said Tess. "I just wish—"

But at that moment, the other two women returned bearing platters of food, so Tess was spared having to complete the thought out loud.

I just wish it would untie that knot in my stomach.

The First Secret

APPRECIATE

Look for specific things about your partner that you love, and when you notice them, take a moment to tell them.

5. Susurrus

The silence that fell at the conclusion of Jeremiah's little princess-and-the-tree story couldn't have lasted more than ten seconds, but to Tom it felt like ten hours. Should he say something? Or wait for the COO to continue?

The longer they sat, the more apparent it became that Jeremiah was not about to break the silence. Finally, Tom decided he had to speak up.

"So . . . I'm guessing, they all lived happily ever after, The End?"

Jeremiah gave him a stern glare.

"This is not a fairy tale, Tom, it's a fable. Not an adventure story, perhaps, but a story, as you put it, with *meaning*." He tilted his head forward expectantly.

Was Tom supposed to interpret the story's "meaning"?

"Um," he began, and then stopped.

"The young man gave her a gift," Jeremiah prompted.

"The dozen roses?"

"No, the tree gave her that. What the young man gave her was his *appreciation*."

"His appreciation," repeated Tom, then he slowly nodded. *Not trinkets or toys*, Jeremiah had said. *Genuine gifts*. "He told her she was very thoughtful."

"The most thoughtful person he'd ever known," corrected Jeremiah. He settled back onto his perch, and before Tom could say another word, he launched back into his story . . .

After that first anniversary, every few days the princess would say to the young man, "Tell me what you love about me," or "You know what I love about you?" and then he would think about it and tell her something new that he loved about her, or he would say, "No, what?" and she would tell him something new that she loved about him.

Soon more flowers appeared on their tree—and not only roses. One by one, all manner of flowers emerged on the little tree's branches: orchids, morning glories, lilies of the valley, and more. An entire forest of flowers, growing from this one tree.

The young man and his bride just shook their heads in amazement. Impossible!

The little tree flourished all through the fall and winter. Soon the spring storms came again, some of them quite fierce indeed. But the flowers survived, and when the breeze rustled and whispered through the leaves at night, now the flowers added their own delicate voices.

"Do you know the word *susurrus*?" the princess said one day when the young man arrived home. She loved learning new words.

"No, I don't," he said. "What does it mean?"

"It means that." She pointed out the window. "What we're hearing. A whispering, like the wind in the leaves. That's *susurrus*."

Susurrus. The young man thought it was the perfect word. That was exactly what it was. A susurrus of sound.

But what was it saying?

On the morning of their second anniversary, the princess was awakened by the smell of cinnamon—her favorite scent. She opened her eyes. The young man had brought her a cup of hot cinnamon tea in bed.

"What's this?"

"Tea," he said.

"I know it's tea. But why did you bring it?"

"I thought you might like it."

She took a hot sip and looked at him, her eyes shining.

"No one has ever brought me hot tea first thing, ever. And this is my favorite tea in the world. How did you know?"

He shrugged. "You must have told me."

But she was sure she had not.

She took a second sip. It seemed to her the most delicious thing she had ever tasted.

The young man kissed her and went off to build roads and bridges.

When he came home late that afternoon and approached the tree, he was astonished at what he saw.

Blueberries!

Blueberries and strawberries and raspberries and huckleberries . . . oranges, lemons and limes, kiwis and kumquats, pears, pomegranates and persimmons—fruit and more fruit, bursting out everywhere among the flowers on every branch, all the new scents mingling with the blossoms to create what the young man was sure must be the most beautiful aroma in the universe.

Their little tree was truly miraculous!

He went to tell the princess, but before he reached the front door it opened and she stepped out, her eyes wide, and said, "I know!"

The two stood together at their door, marveling at the wonder of it.

That evening, the princess asked him if his shoulders hurt. In fact, he admitted, they ached a good deal. (He had worked very hard that day.)

"Sit down here, on the edge of the bed," she commanded. So he did, and she began kneading his shoulders. It was heaven.

"How did you know they ached?" he said. He was sure he hadn't mentioned this; he hadn't wanted to be the kind of husband who complained and talked about himself.

She just smiled and kept working on his neck.

Soon she had massaged the ache away.

Every morning the young man brought his wife hot cinnamon tea, and she painted, and he built, and every evening she massaged the ache from his shoulders.

The little tree grew taller.

"The cinnamon tea was another gift," ventured Tom.

Jeremiah frowned. "Noticing that she loved hot tea in the morning, noticing that she loved the taste of cinnamon, bringing her something he knew she would love—*that* was the gift. The gift of *paying attention.*"

And with that he resumed his story . . .

For their third anniversary, the two had planned another late-afternoon picnic dinner—but it was a drizzly day, and when the young man arrived home, he found a half-finished painting in the living room, smeared and drying. His wife was in bed, sobbing. She had drawn the curtains and the room was dark.

The young man was alarmed.

"Are you okay?" he said.

"No, I'm not okay! If I were okay, would I be here in bed?"

He said quietly, "What's wrong?"

"Everything. Nothing went right today. I can't get the painting right. And now I've ruined our anniversary!"

He went out into the kitchen.

It was dark. There was nothing on the stove.

The young man didn't know what to do.

He went back to the bedroom, where the princess was still quietly sobbing. He started to tell her she was the most thoughtful person he'd ever known, but something stopped him.

He asked if she wouldn't like some hot cinnamon tea, but she just shook her head.

He went out to their kitchen, prepared a little soup, and brought it to her on a tray. "I'm sure the painting will turn out all right," he said.

"I don't see how," she said. She wouldn't even look at him.

He went to sleep that night feeling bad for her and wondering if he had said or done something wrong that made her so upset.

When he awoke the next morning, the young princess had already pulled back the shades and let in the sun. She came and sat at the foot of the bed.

"Thank you for being so sweet last night," she said. "I know you're right. The painting will be okay. The soup was delicious."

He knew the soup was not at all delicious. He was a builder, not a chef.

"You're very kind," he said.

"*You're* very kind," she replied. "Thank you for being so understanding."

He wasn't sure he understood at all, but he was happy to see her in a sunny mood again.

"I'm sorry I snapped at you," she said. "I didn't mean what I said."

The young man squeezed her hand. "I know." This, he did understand. There'd been times when he'd said things he didn't mean, too.

When he stepped out the front door to go off to work, it suddenly struck him that in the three years they had been married and living in their little cottage, he had never seen a bird in their tree, not once.

The reason that thought struck him just then was simply this: now he *was* seeing a bird there.

A lot of birds.

Two dozen, three dozen, maybe four dozen of them—hornbills and hummingbirds, toucans and terns, a charm of finches, a chattering of starlings, a family of bald eagles.

He stood openmouthed for a full minute.

Would their little tree never cease to amaze them?

That night the young man lay in bed next to his wife, listening to the susurrus of wind and leaves and birdsong murmuring well into the night.

Suuussurrrrusssssss . . .

When he awoke the next morning, he thought he had dreamed that he understood its words, and while he could not remember the dream now that he was awake, he felt it was the most restful sleep he had ever had.

Jeremiah finished speaking and sat again in that expectant pose.

Tom glanced down at what he'd just sketched: a little tree at night, its branches waving in the breeze, whispering secrets.

"So," Tom began, "each anniversary there's something new in the tree, and some new element in their relationship. He tells her she's thoughtful, he brings her the tea, he makes her the soup. And the tree. There's some kind of magic happening with the tree."

Jeremiah just sat, eyeing him like an owl.

Tom looked back at his sketch and frowned. "What am I not seeing?"

Jeremiah cocked his head. "Did you already know the word *susurrus*?"

"No," said Tom. "I'd not heard that before."

"Well, then. You've learned at least one new thing today."

Tom was not sure how to take that. He had no idea when Jeremiah was serious and when he was joking.

"Susurrus," added Jeremiah, "is the language of love."

"The language of love," repeated Tom.

Okay.

But what was it saying?

6. Gillian's Story

"How's the kidnap victim?" said Gillian as she set down a tray of the most delicious-smelling finger foods and took a seat across from Tess. "She looks a little shell-shocked." Gillian took a bite of a Manchego empanada, closed her eyes, and groaned. "Ahh . . . Sofia! The woman is an artist."

"A magician," Nicole agreed.

"They were just telling me," said Tess, "about the five secrets of love."

"Five Secrets to *Lasting* Love," said Dee.

"Right," said Tess. "That."

Nicole raised her hand over her head and pointed down at herself. "First Secret," she said.

"Well," said Gillian, who had already polished off her empanada, "I can tell you all about *número dos*. I learned that one from my divorce."

Gillian Waters had married in her early twenties—a marriage that didn't last long.

"Long enough to have a daughter, though," she said. "And I was determined never to put her through that kind of drama, not ever again. So I stayed stupendously single for years." She sighed. "Then I met Jackson."

The two were on opposing sides of a tough business nego-tiation ("Mortal enemies: the perfect start"). To their mutual surprise, they'd concluded the standoff by going into business together. Over the following few years, they got to know each other as business partners.

"The more time I spent with him, the more I enjoyed his com-pany. It never occurred to me that it would get serious." She took a sip of her iced tea. "Ha."

One evening, the two of them went out to dinner to celebrate the third anniversary of the partnership. Jackson gave her a little gift.

"It was a pair of silver earrings," said Gillian. "Not expensive or fancy or anything, just simple little things. And sitting right there in the middle of the restaurant, I burst into tears! Poor Jack-son was mortified, and I was so embarrassed I wanted to crawl under the table. I thanked him, of course, and we went on as if nothing had happened."

"But something had happened," said Tess.

"Oh, yeah. Something had happened, all right. And it freaked me right out. That night Bo—my daughter, all of thirteen at this point—comes into my bedroom. She knew I'd been crying. She sits on the edge of my bed, with her big solemn eyes, and says, 'Mom, you should marry Jackson.'"

"Whoa," said Tess.

"Yeah. I just about wet the bed. 'Why, Bo-bird?' I said.

"'Because,' she said. 'He makes you happy.'"

Gillian wiped her eyes, uttered a mild curse under her breath, and blew her nose on her napkin. "How on earth she knew that, I have no clue. *I* didn't even know it yet!"

Nicole laughed; Dee chuckled; Melanie smiled.

Tess smiled, too. She wondered if she could arrange for Jamie and Bo to meet sometime. Bo sounded like she might be a wise little soul, too.

"But she was right," Gillian continued. "I was in love with this guy—and that terrified me. I'd already failed at marriage once. What was to say I wouldn't fail again? So I went to see this famous marriage coach a friend told me about. Five minutes into the second session, I got it."

It was when the professor began explaining the Second Secret that Gillian's insight struck.

"In the first session, we'd already covered *número uno*." She looked at Tess. "Which was . . . ?"

"Appreciate," said Tess.

"Bingo." Gillian grinned. "Just checking." She took another sip of iced tea with one hand and held up two fingers with the other. "So, secret number two: *attend*."

"Attend," Tess repeated. "Meaning . . . ?"

"To attend, as the professor explained it, means to be present. To be there for the other person. To attend to someone means to take care of them. Tune to them. See what they need, sense what they want, notice what they love. It means to *pay attention*. Not just to appreciate them, but to let them *feel* that appreciation through some meaningful, tangible action.

"And that doesn't have to be some big dramatic gesture. Sometimes, the professor pointed out, the most romantic thing is the smallest thing. What makes it romantic is that you notice it matters to the other person—and you do something about it.

"And that's when it clicked."

Gillian polished off her tea and held her glass out to Dee for a refill as she talked.

"Not long after the divorce, Bo and I had adopted a stray cat we named Cleo. Every now and then, Cleo would show her devotion by leaving a dead mouse on the doorstep."

"Lovely," said Tess. Dee chuckled.

"Yeah," said Gillian. "Cleo's concept of thoughtful gift giving. Craig used to do that, too. Give me things that were his concept of a great gift. His—not necessarily mine. Jewelry, for example.

"Craig liked to give me jewelry. I am not a big jewelry person, but sometimes I like to put on something simple and elegant. One Christmas, when our marriage was starting to come apart, he gave me this big expensive gold necklace." She shook her head. "Craig always went with gold. I don't like gold. It's just not my color."

"Your color is silver," murmured Tess.

Gillian looked at Tess and nodded slowly. "Bingo," she said again. "I've always been a silver girl." Now her voice dropped nearly to a whisper. "But here's the thing. How did Jackson know that?" She shook her head, as if it still mystified her. "I asked him once. He just shrugged and said, 'I don't know. You must have mentioned it.' But I'm sure I didn't."

"He paid attention," said Tess.

Again, Gillian looked over at Tess and nodded that slow nod. "That's exactly right. He paid attention."

"And that's why you burst into tears."

Gillian took a big breath. "Yup. Someone was actually interested in me—interested enough to pick up on the fact that I liked silver. It was a brand-new experience, and it just about leveled me.

"And it's not just gifts. He notices things. What I like, what I don't like. He's an early riser—which I am decidedly not—and instead of giving me grief about it, he slips out early and lets me sleep. In fact, he also knows that once I do wake up, I like to sit in bed in the morning with a hot cup of coffee and read the news. So what does he do? Without a word, he shows up with a cup of hot coffee! The good stuff!"

She shook her head. "No one should be that thoughtful. I mean, it's practically criminal."

Dee chortled; Nicole laughed out loud.

Gillian got quiet again for a moment. "The professor said something else in that session, something I thought about all the way home that day and all that week. I still think about it today. 'To really attend to someone,' she said, 'you have to be interested enough in them to find out what they need, want, and love. To do so day in and day out? For years on end? You have to be *fascinated* with that person! And here's the beautiful thing about this: The more you learn, the more there is to know. Every individual is an unexplored continent.'

"And that," Gillian concluded, "is what I never had with Craig. He never seemed all that interested in exploring who I was. He was in love with me, but I'm not sure he ever really liked me."

"And Jackson?" Nicole prompted.

Gillian smiled. "Best friend I've ever had."

But Tess was no longer listening. She was thinking about that last thing the professor had said.

47

Every individual is an unexplored continent.

It reminded her of that first day in Ecuador, when she and Tom had talked into the night, and how for the next two years, they used to go on long walks and talk about anything and everything. They would talk about their childhoods, what was going on at Rachel's, and their future dreams and plans. Tom would tell Tess about books he'd read, stories he'd loved growing up, sometimes stories he imagined himself writing someday, until he would stop and say, "You must be getting tired of hearing about this." And Tess would always smile and say, "Tell me more."

When was the last time they did that?

Dee nudged Tess. "You okay on time?"

Tess glanced at her phone and nodded. "Got a little while still."

"Let's see if we can cover all Five Secrets before you have to go," said Dee. "Which means number three is next."

She looked over at Melanie. "Mel?"

Tess realized that up to this point, she had not heard the third woman utter a single word.

The Second Secret

ATTEND

Convey your love through some meaningful, tangible action. Pay attention. Notice what your partner needs, wants, and loves, then give them that.

7. Melanie's Story

Melanie took a slow, thoughtful sip from her glass, then set it down carefully.

"So, years ago," she began, "my husband and I had a child who died. It nearly destroyed our marriage."

She paused, and Tess felt her heart clench.

"Ben and I had very different ways of grieving," Mel continued softly. "He wanted to have another child right away. I couldn't bear the thought. He was very sweet with me, but after a year I could see he was losing patience. And I was feeling more and more alone. We went to see the professor. Separately, not together, though we compared notes later.

"The professor said, 'You're both fighting a battle right now, and it's one of the toughest ones there is. The question is, are you on the same team? Or are you like the cowboys who circle their wagons and shoot inward? When you draw your battle lines, do you draw them around the two of you—or between you?'"

Mel paused to take another sip before continuing. There was no sound from the others. It seemed to Tess that even the birds in the expanse of yard beyond them had stilled their voices, giving Mel the space to speak.

"Then the professor told me about the four deadliest words in marriage: I love you, *but* . . .

"I love you, *but* I'd love you more if you would be just a little different in this or that particular way. I love you, *but* I wish you would exercise more, or take out the trash, or spend less, or whatever. I love you, *but* I'd love you more if you'd be just a little stronger, a little slimmer, a little more assertive, a little more accepting—and with those four little words, pretty soon you've invented this entire fictional character who is not the person sitting next to you and never will be."

Mel said the professor told her that the path through her battle, the path out of pain, was to be fully with the person you were with—the actual person, just the way they were.

"That, according to the professor, was what the Third Secret was all about."

Mel took another sip of tea and continued.

"'The Third Secret,' said the professor, 'is about having a generous spirit. About always assuming the other person means well. Embracing forgiveness and acceptance as your default mode. The Third Secret says, when in doubt, be kind. Being kind means taking responsibility for the energy you bring to the relationship, and not saying harsh or hurtful things. Not even thinking them, if you can manage that. The Third Secret asks you to become aware of your words and thoughts, and then bend their arc toward *allowance*.

"'In a word, Melanie, child, the Third Secret is to *allow*.'"

"Allow?" Tess hated to interrupt Mel's story, but she wanted to make sure she understood the professor's point. "How so? Allow what?"

"Allow the other person to be the way they are," explained Mel. "To be *who* they are.

"The professor said people often don't see how important this is until they're faced with a crisis, which is typically when couples pull together . . . or pull apart. Which way you go, and whether your relationship survives, will depend largely on how you've been treating each other during the rosier times.

"And then she added something that hit me like a punch in the gut. 'So now, Melanie, child, you have to ask yourself, what kind of marriage do you have? What kind of marriage do you want?'"

Tess thought about her and Tom's own struggles with all of Jamie's issues. They seemed almost trivial in comparison to what Mel had gone through. The death of a child—she couldn't even imagine it. Although there'd been moments when she *had* imagined it, many moments, actually, when she was terrified that Jamie would not be okay, that they would lose him. It had been a battle every inch of the way.

But they had hung together through the hard times, hadn't they?

They'd never circled their wagons and shot inward . . . had they?

"After our first child died," Mel was saying, "I couldn't talk on the phone. I mean, not to anyone. I don't know why, I just couldn't. So Ben did. Whether it was the plumber, or the bank, or friends, or whoever, Ben took the call.

"When I explained this, the professor nodded and said, 'Allowing means sometimes you take on each other's burdens. Who cooks? Who pays the bills? Who keeps up the laundry? You fill in whatever gaps need filling—and you never, ever keep score. Because a fifty-fifty marriage is a formula for failure.'

"Allowing, I learned, means you throw out the scorecard."

Mel took one more sip of tea before continuing in the same hushed tone.

"We did have another child, eventually. A boy, Robbie. He just turned twenty-one, and he's already executive chef at a great restaurant here in the center of town."

She smiled with pride, then grew pensive again.

"I don't think we would have made it, though, without the Third Secret.

"I still remember, word for word, what the professor said at the end of that first session: 'The world can be a hard place, full of treachery and heartbreak. Be his refuge, his sanctuary, his safe harbor from the stings of the world. And let him be the same for you.'"

Tess sat still, the professor's words crashing through her mind like peals of thunder.

Be his refuge, his safe harbor from the stings of the world—and let him be the same for you.

After Jamie was born, Tess tore into the job of caring for him like a mother bear. Tom threw himself into advancement at work in hopes of hacking away at their growing mountain of medical bills (a mountain they'd yet to summit). He even went as far as taking on a position that had him constantly crisscrossing the country.

Tess had missed work terribly—and Tom sorely missed spending time with their son. They'd both struggled . . . but had their struggles drawn them closer together? Or pulled them apart?

Had Tom been her refuge? Had she been his?

Or had they each retreated to their own corners?

Tess looked up from her reverie. All of a sudden, the other women were on their feet, rushing about, collecting the glassware and dishes as a mounting wind whipped through the terrace. The sky had gone dark.

A storm was gathering.

Tess hurriedly tapped out a short text message for Tom, and then hesitated, her thumb over the SEND button. Right now, he would be in the midst of the most important interview of his life. She shouldn't interrupt, not even with a one-line text. *Probably has his phone shut off*, she thought. *Probably he won't even see it till later.*

She almost deleted it, but instead she pressed SEND:

> You're a great father.

Then she grabbed her plate and followed the others inside, shutting the door just as a sheet of rain swept across the terrace and crashed into the stone mansion.

The Third Secret

ALLOW

Take responsibility for the energy you bring to the relationship. Accept your partner for who they are, the way they are. Be their safe harbor. Have a generous spirit. Be kind.

8. The Storm

The storm slammed into the building and sheets of rain shattered over the plate-glass windows, bringing Jeremiah to his feet. Tom assumed he meant to close the blinds and switch on more lighting—but instead he did the opposite, opening the blinds the rest of the way and switching *off* the few lights that were already on. Soon the room was bathed in the dark purple-gray tinge of a torrential spring squall.

Tom felt his phone buzz in his pocket and silently chided himself. How had he neglected to shut it off before walking into this interview?

Slipping the phone out, he snuck a peek before switching off the ringer. It was a text message from Tess.

> You're a great father.

Tom felt his breath catch. Where did *that* come from? Had Tess ever told him that before? He was pretty sure she hadn't.

Was it true?

He certainly wanted it to be true. Throughout their ordeal, Tess had always been there for Jamie. Tess had been amazing. And Tom? He wanted to be a good father, every bit as much as he

59

wanted to be a good husband. But he felt like he was missing his own kid's life.

He looked up and realized that Jeremiah had gone still, watching Tom. The older man gave a small nod, whose exact meaning Tom could not interpret, then retook his seat and resumed his narrative as if there had been no interruption at all.

"The fourth year," said Jeremiah. "Now, the fourth year was more difficult . . ."

When the spring storms came that year, they were fiercer than ever before. Hailstones the size of plums fell all about, and in between the storms there were earth tremors. The little tree was badly damaged. Still, the young couple was grateful it wasn't worse. Many other older, larger trees were uprooted and destroyed.

The terrible weather worsened through May, pushing right up to June's front door. By the time their next anniversary arrived, a picnic was out of the question.

That evening they sat up on their bed, eating a cold dinner by candlelight.

"Tell me something," said the princess.

"About what?" said the young man.

"Tell me something about you."

"What about me? You already know everything."

She shook her head. "I know almost nothing. What's the last thing you think about before you sleep? The first thing you think of when you wake? What frightened you as a child? What are your deepest secrets, your darkest fears?"

The young man didn't know where to start.

"What's something you've never told anyone else?" she said.

The young man thought for a long minute, then began to speak.

"At school, there was a girl in my class who used to make fun of me. She made fun of everyone, actually; nobody liked her. One day I got upset and pushed her down. She got a cut on her face and cried; she had to get stitches."

The princess said nothing.

"No one saw me do it," the young man continued. "And I said another boy did it because she'd teased him. Nobody liked this particular boy, either, so everyone believed me. She and the other boy were both punished. I never told anyone what really happened. I was so ashamed. I felt terrible about it. I still feel terrible."

The princess was silent.

"It wasn't okay, what I did," he said.

"No," she agreed.

"It was bad."

She squeezed his hand. "It was. But that doesn't make you a bad person."

He looked at her, then looked away again. "Thank you for listening."

"Thank you for telling me."

"Does it make you love me less?"

She smiled. "It makes me love you more." She took his hand and rested her head on his shoulder, and they drifted off to sleep just like that as the storm raged on.

Tom gazed out at the rain, replaying the princess's words to her young husband.

What's the last thing you think about before you sleep? The first thing you think of when you wake? What frightened you as a child? What are your deepest secrets, your darkest fears?

The questions begat more questions.

What was Tess's first-grade teacher's name?

What was her favorite book in grade school?

How did her first pet die?

When was the first time she ever felt ashamed, and why?

These questions all struck him as extraordinarily intimate—and he didn't know the answer to a single one of them.

And what about his own deepest, darkest secrets, those things he'd never told anyone? Had he ever shared them with her?

He thought about that first day in Ecuador, how they'd talked into the night, and how nervous he'd been that he was going on for too long about himself. But she'd kept laughing and smiling and saying, "Tell me more."

Tess was a lot like the princess in Jeremiah's story. She always wanted to hear what he had to say, no matter how half-formed or unsure his thoughts might be. They would take long walks and talk about everything under the sun, and yet there was always still more to talk about the next time.

Tell me more. It had been the tagline of their relationship.

When was the last time she'd said that?

Suddenly it seemed like ages since they'd really talked.

Outside the plate-glass window the storm howled on, but the room around them was silent. Tom looked over at Jeremiah, who was patiently waiting.

"Telling her that secret," said Tom. "That was another gift."

Jeremiah nodded. "It was."

The young man was awakened the next morning by the most beautiful sound he'd ever heard. It seemed to be coming from outside, from the direction of their tree—but it was unlike any sound he'd heard before, not a rustling and whispering, but a delicate jingling, like a band of fairies dancing with little bells on their fingers and toes.

Now his bride opened her eyes, too.

He put his finger to his lips.

She nodded and followed him silently out to the front yard, where they stopped and stared.

Somehow, the little tree's leaves had turned to pure gold and silver, transforming into the most beautiful wind chimes in the world.

The susurrus had become a symphony.

He still could not tell what it said—but it was saying it more gloriously than any music he had ever heard.

"I didn't know you were a *magic* princess," he said.

"I didn't either," she said. She looked at him, then again at the tree. "Maybe it wasn't me."

The young man said nothing. *It had to be you*, he thought. *Who else could it be?*

"But it wasn't her, was it," said Tom.

"Hmm?" said Jeremiah.

"It wasn't her. Or him. It was *them*."

Jeremiah raised his eyebrows but said nothing.

"The tree," said Tom. "The tree is marriage itself, isn't it?"

Jeremiah sat back on his perch. "That particular tree," he said, "is their particular marriage. It's different for everyone.

"Tolstoy famously wrote that happy families are all alike, while every unhappy family is unhappy in its own way. In my observation, the opposite is true. Every unhappy couple is unhappy in precisely the same way: their tree has withered and begun to die.

"But every happy couple? Well, now, they each trace their own particular pathways to happiness, don't they. Their own words and deeds, acts of kindness, gestures of empathy. The walks taken, confidences shared, favorite colors noted. Chores done preemptively. Hot cups of tea served in bed. Different as fingerprints."

Tom thought for a moment. Then he said, "Their own gifts."

"Their own gifts," agreed Jeremiah.

What kind of tree, Tom wondered, did he and Tess have?

And how was it doing?

9. The Professor

As the others moved farther into the kitchen and away from the raging storm outside, Tess took a moment to absorb her surroundings. The place was at once homey and magnificent, all vaulted ceilings, gleaming surfaces, and rich, warming aromas. Over by the stove stood a child, her back to them, portioning out something hot into widemouthed earthen bowls.

"Sofia, OMG," exclaimed Gillian. "What *is* that? It smells like heaven on a spoon!"

Tess just had time to wonder whose daughter (or granddaughter?) this was when Sofia turned with her loaded tray, and Tess saw that she was not a child at all but a woman in her . . . fifties? Sixties?

"Sofia," said Dee, "this is Tess. Tess, meet Sofia."

The cook beamed a smile at them. "Paella," she replied to Gillian. To Tess she gave a nod and the hint of a curtsy, which somewhat terrified Tess, given that the tiny woman held a tray full of piping-hot food that had to weigh nearly as much as she did. "Lovely to meet you, Tess," she said, her words rich with the lilt and snap of a Castilian accent. *Luffly to meet you, Taysss.*

"Sit, sit, sit!" Sofia said to the others. *Seet, seet, seet!* Strands of white hair shook loose from her headscarf as she moved, and

Tess promptly gave up trying to guess the cook's age. She might have been anywhere from forty-five to eighty-five. Or altogether ageless.

Tess sat down with the others as the cook set the steaming bowls before them. Gillian was right; it did smell like heaven on a spoon—and tasted like it, too. She wished she could inhale the whole bowl. As it was, she managed only a few bites before that knot in her stomach forced her to stop.

The others dug in as the storm hammered the glass behind them. Sofia watched Tess not eating.

"The paella is incredible," said Tess, feeling guilty that she had barely touched it.

"Stratospheric," commented Gillian, which made Melanie smile.

"Gracias," said Sofia with a little bow of her head. "Very kind." She now took a seat herself, next to Tess. After a moment she said, "So, Tess. What brings you here?"

"Dee kidnapped her," said Gillian, shaking her head sorrowfully. "Felonious Dee." That brought another smile from Mel, and one from Tess as well.

"Actually," Tess confided to Sofia, "I think it's more like she rescued me. I was having a bad day."

"Yes," said Sofia.

There was something strangely comforting, almost hypnotic, in that single word. *Yaysss*. It was as if the woman was perfectly content with that vague explanation, yet equally willing to listen to further commentary on whatever lay beneath, if Tess chose to offer it.

"Oh," said Tess as the penny dropped.

Sofia was not the household cook. She was the professor—the person Tess had been hearing about for the past hour!

And without really intending to, or even knowing why she was doing it, Tess began to talk.

She told Sofia—the professor—all about Jamie, about their trials and tribulations, the years of searching out the therapies and support he needed, about Tom's job and the stress of his constant travel. She detailed his day of crucial interviews, happening even now as she sat in that cozy kitchen talking while the storm outside howled.

As Tess unburdened herself, Sofia listened. Finally, when Tess paused after describing the trouble at Jamie's school that morning, Sofia spoke up.

"So, you used to work there, too. At the coffee company."

Tess nodded.

"Your man . . ."

"Tom," put in Tess.

"Tom. Does Tom know how hard this has been for you?"

"Oh, believe me," Tess replied, "it's been hard for him, too, incredibly hard. In a way even harder, maybe, because he's had to leave so much of it all to me. And he loves that little boy so much."

Tears stung her eyes as she thought about putting Jamie to bed on those nights when Tom was on the road, about Jamie saying, "Papa?" and Tess saying, "Tomorrow, baby," or "In two days, baby," or "This weekend, baby." And the mornings when he woke up all bright-eyed and eager, and Tess knew what his first word would be before he uttered it—"Papa?"

It made her heart ache.

Lord, how she hoped Tom would land that COO position today, so he could actually be home for a change.

"I'm sure," said Sofia. "But that wasn't my question."

Tess blinked. "I'm sorry," she said. "What . . ." Her thoughts had so churned her up that she couldn't remember exactly where their conversation had left off. "What was your question again?"

Sofia touched Tess's sleeve and said, "Does he know—really know—how hard this has been for you?"

Tess started to reply, but stopped herself.

Did he know? Of course he did. He had to know. After all they'd gone through together? He must.

"Tess?" said Sofia. "Let's do something, if you like. I ask a question, a personal question—but you don't answer it, not out loud, not to me or anyone else. Just to yourself. Yes?"

"Okay," said Tess uncertainly.

"What have you not told Tom? What is there, maybe something you're a little bit ashamed of, that you've never told anyone? Maybe not even yourself?"

Tess sat back and looked down at her folded hands.

Something she'd never told anyone—not even herself?

She couldn't think of a thing.

Tess did not have any deep, dark secrets. There were no skeletons in her closet. Her closet was too crowded for any skeletons to fit in there anyway, jam-packed as it was with all those clothes, outfits she hadn't worn in years and probably never would at this rate—nice skirts, silk blouses, business suits, that sharp-looking, all-purpose jacket she used to take with her everywhere when she and Tom would visit supplier-partners and their families—

"Oh," she gasped, and one hand flew to her mouth as if she'd just seen something horrifying.

Which, in a way, she had.

All at once it had struck her: just how much she resented their situation.

The day they had made their big decision, the one she thought of as Worst Day Ever, it had stormed all afternoon and deep into the night. For a few hours, the power went out, and Tess remembered sitting in the dark, eating a gloomy dinner by candlelight, thinking about how that ought to be romantic . . . and how it felt the very opposite of romantic.

She missed the work, missed it more than she'd ever really admitted—not to Tom, not even to herself. She resented the fact that Tom got to go to work every day at a company she dearly loved while she was stuck at home with the cares and woes of family. And she felt horribly, titanically guilty for feeling that way. For even thinking it. But there it was.

Did she take it out on Tom? She didn't think so, but . . . maybe she did.

No, she definitely did.

Her thoughts flew back to that morning, to her frantic efforts to get Jamie ready while planning for her conference call in her head . . . Tom being so preoccupied with his coming interview that he was no help at all . . . her getting irritated at him . . . him retreating further as he felt her bristle . . .

"Oh, Lord," she murmured. She looked up at Sofia. "This is something we have to work on."

The professor shook her head gently.

"No?" said Tess.

"This is something *you* have to work on, *cariño.*"

"Just me? But . . . I think it's both of us."

Sofia glanced around the table. "Have they told you about the 5 Secrets?"

"Just the first three," put in Dee.

"Okey-doke," said Sofia, the unlikely words sounding like a magical incantation when she spoke them.

"My first year in private practice, I listened to many, many couples bring their dramas into the therapy room. Each person was an expert in what was wrong with the other, what was wrong with the marriage, why his grievances or her grievances were clearly a harder burden to bear." She sighed. "It was like watching American daytime TV."

Gillian snorted a laugh.

"So I shut my practice down for a month, which turned into a year. I changed how I thought about my practice. When I began again, I no longer called myself a 'couples therapist.' Instead, I now worked as a *marriage coach*. Also—and this was the key, *cariño*—I started seeing people singly, one at a time. I began focusing each person on what *they* could do.

"The challenge with most couples therapy is that it's too easy to focus on what's 'wrong' with the other person—what they're

doing, or not doing, or should be doing. But that only perpetu-
ates the drama. You cannot change the other person. The only one
you can change, *cariño*, is you.

"To really work on a marriage, you don't work on the
marriage—you work on yourself. And trust your partner to do
the same."

Tess looked out the sliding glass doors at the rain. "What if
they don't?" she said.

Sofia smiled. "Well, Tess. You hope they do. But some things
are out of your control. Most things."

Tess was silent. That sounded so hopeless. She thought about
Amy and Alex and their "amicable divorce." This all must have
showed on her face, because Sofia suddenly erupted in laughter
and patted Tess on the arm.

"It's not so bad!" she said. "In fact, it's very good. Because
while you cannot change another person, you do have a secret
weapon."

"I do?"

"You do." Sofia leaned closer and said softly: "Your belief."

"My belief in . . . ?"

"In him. In Tom. These are the two great sources of strength
and resilience in a marriage. Your belief in him. And his belief in
you."

From across the table, Melanie caught Tess's eye and mouthed
the words *Fourth Secret*.

"Your unwavering belief in your partner is perhaps the most
powerful gift you can give," the professor continued. "Your
faith in each other is what builds the soil of your relationship.

It is what fosters trust between the two of you. And trust is as essential to a durable relationship as love. As long as you don't fully trust each other, you're still two separate parties locked in a long-term negotiation. And in a marriage, there is nothing more painful than isolation."

Sofia paused to let her words sink in. When she spoke again, her voice was softer still.

"But when you believe in someone you love? Really fully believe in them? Miraculous things take root. Give your complete, unshakable faith and trust to another and you equip them with the tools they need to fight life's most arduous battles. When the two of you are truly on each other's team, there is nothing the world can throw at you that you cannot handle."

"Paella!" a voice exclaimed from across the room. "My favorite!"

Everyone turned to see a tall, slender man with neatly combed snow-white hair, a pale blue shirt, and pressed light-gray slacks enter the kitchen from the interior of the house.

"Mind if I join?" he said. He leaned down and kissed Sofia's upturned face, first on one cheek, then the other.

"Tess," said Gillian, "meet Mister Sofia."

The man let out a booming laugh. "Mister Sofia! I love that. I think I'll put that on my business cards!"

He took the lone remaining empty seat, the one on the other side of Tess, as Nicole quietly stepped over to the stove to bring him a bowl of paella.

"And it's quite appropriate, you know," he said to Tess. "Everything I know about marriage, about life, I learned from Sofia."

The professor nodded. "This is true. I have taught him every-thing worth knowing. Of course, first I learned it from him."

Tess glanced at her sharply to see if she was joking. It was impossible to tell.

"How did you—" she started to ask, but at that moment the rain stopped as abruptly as it had started.

Dee caught Tess's eye, and Tess remembered that they were on the clock. Reluctantly, she nodded and stood. Time to go.

It looked like she wouldn't get to hear about the Fifth Secret after all.

The Fourth Secret

BELIEVE

Believe in your partner wholeheartedly. Give them your complete, unshakable trust. Let your faith show.

10. The Purpose of Marriage

Jeremiah stood looking out the big plate-glass window at the distant rolling mountains. The passing storm had scrubbed the air and made the outlines stark, the colors vivid.

His back still to Tom, he spoke.

The fifth year, there were no spring storms at all. Instead, the weeks of March and April were wrung dry by a long, slow drought. This, to everyone's shock and dismay, was followed by a deep freeze that stretched its icy fingers clear across the month of May.

At night, the young man heard nothing but a pale wind whistling over the land . . .

Jeremiah glanced back over his shoulder at Tom.

"I've seen marriages like that," he said. "Perhaps you have, too. No big storms. No thunder, no earth tremors. Just a long, silent freeze that squeezes the life out of the thing, squeezes it to the point where an actual declaration of death would be a mere formality."

He turned back to gaze again at the mountains.

Tom shuddered. Yes, he had known people in marriages like that. It was something he had always sworn would never happen to him and Tess.

As their fifth anniversary approached, the little tree began to sag. Its leaves lost their luster, gold turning to copper, silver to tin. One day the young man reached up to feel one leaf. It crumpled at his touch.

They had all turned to tissue paper.

The birds, too, began to fade, their feathers turning a thin, translucent gray, their diverse songs all dissolving into the same simple call, repeating over and over again: "Ka-*kaw*, ka-*kaw*. Ka-*kaw*, ka-*kaw* . . ."

It's like the first year, he told himself. *That's all. It'll get better by itself. Maybe on our anniversary.*

He told himself these things but knew they were not true.

By now he understood that it was their own behavior that determined the state of their little tree. It had survived terrible storms and horrific earthquakes because of their love for each other. If it was going to survive this terrible freeze, it would be up to them.

So he redoubled his efforts.

Every day, he found more things he loved about the princess and told her how much he appreciated them.

He made her favorite snacks and brought her some beautiful pieces of fine canvas for her landscapes.

He did everything he could think of, but the tree only continued to fail. At night, through the window, he could hear its branches rattling in the wind.

One night, as he lay awake long after the princess had gone to sleep, he heard the clatter of twigs outside—even though there was no wind at all.

It sounded like a death rattle.

"Our tree is dying," said the princess.

She had not gone to sleep after all.

"I know," he said.

They both lay in the dark, listening to the twigs' dry rasp and feeling sad. Then she said, "Can I ask you something?"

He smiled. "You can ask me anything."

She said, "Do you love building roads?"

He hesitated. Then he said, "Not really."

"Bridges?"

"No, not bridges either."

It had not occurred to him until that moment, but it was true. He didn't hate what he did, but he didn't truly love it, either.

"Why do you do it?" she said.

"For you. For us. So we can survive."

She was silent for a moment. Then she said, "What is your heart's desire?"

"You are!" the young man said.

"No, silly," she said. "I am your heart's container. I hold your heart in my hands, every day, even when you sleep at night, so that nothing can hurt it. But I can't protect it from hurting itself."

After another moment's silence, she said, "So what is your heart's desire? What do you want to do? Who do you want to be?"

The young man was quiet for a long time. Finally, he said, "Well." He took a breath. "I've always wanted to build a cathedral."

She sat up straight and peered at him through the darkness.

"Really?"

He nodded.

"Wow," she said. She lay back down next to him. "I've always wanted to make a big stained-glass rose window."

The young man lay awake for a long time, imagining his beautiful cathedral with its magnificent multicolored window.

As he dropped off to sleep, he could have sworn he heard a faint murmur rustling in the breeze outside.

By this point in Jeremiah's story, Tom had stopped sketching and closed his eyes. He couldn't stop thinking about himself and Tess.

Was their tree dying?

At some point, when neither of them was looking, the good old days of "Tessandtom" had quietly slipped away. He'd been so consumed with worry about Jamie, so caught up in their mounting financial crisis, that he hadn't even noticed when it happened.

He opened his eyes and looked at Jeremiah.

He had to know how the fable ended.

"You said marriage was all about giving."

Jeremiah nodded, still facing the mountains.

"Their first anniversary," Tom continued, "he told her she was the most thoughtful person he'd ever known. He gave her *appreciation*. The second anniversary, he gave her his *attention*, noticing what she loved. The third, he gave her *space*, I guess."

"*Allowing*," said Jeremiah.

"*Allowing*," repeated Tom, nodding. "Okay. And the fourth, he gave her his *trust*."

"Because she *believed* in him," Jeremiah interjected, "and he knew it. And he in turn believed in her."

"*Belief*." Tom nodded once more. "Okay, I see that. All this, I get. But what exactly was he giving her now? What was the gift that kept their tree from dying?"

Jeremiah paused before he spoke. "I haven't yet said whether it dies or not."

"Of course it doesn't!" Tom nearly shouted. "Of course it lives—they bring it back to life! And live happily ever after, you know they do! My question is how? What was their fifth gift to each other?"

Now Jeremiah turned and looked at Tom.

"When you first came in today," he said, "I asked you five questions. Do you remember what the fifth one was?"

Tom thought back. "You asked me why I wanted this job."

"And you told me it would be good for your family. A fine reason."

Jeremiah walked over to retake his perch as he continued speaking.

"There are plenty of fine reasons people take a job. They need the income. It's something they're good at and, one hopes, enjoy doing, perhaps even love doing. It contributes to the betterment of society. All excellent reasons for pouring your time into a particular channel. But not the best reason." He shook his head. "No, the best reason? The bottom-line purpose of a career? To *become*."

"To become," echoed Tom.

Jeremiah gave a sage nod. "Exactly."

"To become what?"

Jeremiah looked at him as if he'd asked the simplest question in the universe.

"Why, to become Tom, of course."

Tom frowned. He glanced down at his little notebook and found another sketch looking back at him: a tiny brick cottage, and behind it a beautiful little stone cathedral with a magnificent stained-glass rose window high up on its front-facing wall.

He looked back at Jeremiah.

"So all those other questions you asked—what I wanted to be when I grew up, my favorite book, my heroes . . ."

"Clues to who you're seeking to become."

Tom thought back through their earlier conversation. "And then you asked me one more question."

"Ah, yes," said Jeremiah. "The purpose of marriage." He steepled his fingers again and peered at Tom. "The purpose of marriage," he said, "is to give yourself fully to another—and in the process, become your best self."

Tom repeated the words softly to himself.

"The purpose of marriage is to give yourself fully to another—and in the process, become your best self."

He looked up at Jeremiah. "To build your cathedral."

"To build your cathedral." For the first time since their meeting began, Jeremiah's face showed the hint of a smile. "Well put, young man. Well put, indeed."

11. The Fifth Secret

"I'm curious," said Tess, as they drove out of the circular drive and away from the stone mansion. "How do you know the professor?"

"Her name was on my report card," said Dee, smiling. "I got an A." And she gave Tess a quick summary of her story.

Dee started out working in advertising ("For which I had neither great talent nor great love," she added). When she got married, she happily quit her agency job to raise a family. Two and a half decades later, her three kids now grown and on their own, she went back to school to study children's literature and early education.

"Which was where I met Sofia. I was in one of her seminars on family dynamics." She chuckled. "I'll never forget the title of that class. Soil Science and the Ecology of Relationships."

"Wow," said Tess.

Dee laughed. "Yeah. Does that sound like college or what?"

"Seriously. Okay, I'll bite: How does soil science figure into family dynamics? And what exactly is 'the ecology of relationships'?"

Dee grinned. "First class, she handed out a fresh persimmon to every student in the room. We all stared at them. 'Eat, eat, eat!' she said. 'I grew these myself—enjoy them! They're delicious!'

And they were, no question about that. We all sat there, eating our persimmons and wondering what this crazy lady was all about. And she started to talk.

"'When I was a young girl, growing up in Castilla–La Mancha,' she said, 'I had a little persimmon tree out behind our house. One year the fruits were bad, and I asked my father, why? What could I do?

"'He said to me, well, *cariño*, you have to ask, why are they bad?

"'I said, they are bad because bugs found my tree and bored into it.

"'No, *cariño*, my father said, it is the other way around. The bugs came *because* the persimmons were not well. The persimmons were not well because the tree itself was not well. And the tree is not well because of the soil. If the soil is not strong and healthy, the tree cannot be strong and healthy, and nothing good can grow there.

"'So, my friends,' the professor asked us, 'what is the soil of a marriage?'

"We were all silent, of course. None of us knew what the soil of a marriage was.

"She smiled at us and said, 'You are. Marriage is a tree—and you are the soil. If the soil is exhausted and depleted, then nothing can help the marriage. You want to heal a marriage? Feed the soil.'"

Dee took a deep breath and paused before letting it out again. Reliving the scene, Tess realized with surprise, had made the remedial reading teacher rather emotional.

"The moment she said it, I didn't just understand it—I recognized it. After twenty-odd years of raising a family, *I* was exhausted and depleted. My whole life had revolved around taking care of others for so long that I'd lost track of how to take care of myself.

"I had quite a few friends who were going through the same thing. Kids leaving home, house suddenly quiet and empty. Looking in the mirror one morning and realizing there was something missing.

"And this wasn't just about mothers and children. I had friends my age who'd had no children but just poured themselves into their careers, and who arrived at the same sort of midlife crisis, their marriages tired and worn out. Getting divorces or having affairs. Taking pills. Any distraction to avoid the emptiness in the mirror.

"But what was missing was *them*."

They came to a red light. Dee slowed to a stop, then turned and looked over at Tess.

"Some of my friends blamed their marriages for their unhappiness. But that's like the soil blaming the tree."

She paused again, remembering those years.

"Even before Sofia gave me the language to explain it, I knew I had to do something to nourish myself. To reinvent myself. I knew the point of a marriage wasn't simply to raise kids, grow old, and die. A marriage is meant to keep growing. *You* are meant to keep growing.

"In fact, Tess, that right there is the Fifth Secret. *Grow*. Every day. Figure out what you need to be healthy, happy, and fulfilled—and then give yourself that."

The light changed and Dee drove on while Tess pondered what she had said.

"I get the concept," said Tess. "But shouldn't we be getting that, at least to some extent, *from* the marriage?"

"Other way around. You bring that *to* your marriage. If you go into your marriage with an expectation of what you're going to get from it, then you'll drain the life out of it. You can't give from a place of emptiness, exhaustion, or unhappiness. The more you take care of yourself, the more you're able to give to the other person."

She signaled for a right turn, then added, "It's not your job to make your husband happy. And it's not his job to make you happy. That's something we all need to do for ourselves.

"The first four secrets are all about what you give to the other person. You appreciate them. Attend to them. Allow them. Believe in them.

"The Fifth Secret, though—that one is about you. Because to fully love another, you have to fully love yourself."

She brought her car to a stop back in the same spot where they'd started, right next to Tess's car. "And here we are!"

Tess unbuckled her seat belt but didn't move to get out. "Thank you, Dee," she said.

"For what?"

"For kidnapping me."

Dee smiled. "Any time."

Tess opened the car door and put one foot out, then turned back. "Hey, I meant to ask. What exactly is the Marriage Project?"

"Ah," said Dee. "We're making the 5 Secrets into a mobile app. Easier to learn, easier to practice. Nicole is software, Mel's design. Gillian manages infrastructure and distribution. I'm working with Sofia to write all the content."

"A mobile app," echoed Tess. "Changing the world, one marriage at a time?"

Dee smiled. "Something like that. The more marriages we have operating on the Pindar Principle, the happier the world—"

"Wait," Tess interrupted. "The Peter Principle? How does that apply here?"

"Not *Peter*," said Dee. "*Pindar*. Sofia's husband."

Tess pulled her foot back inside and turned fully in her seat to stare at Dee. "That's Pindar? I was just talking to *Pindar*?"

Tess knew very well who Pindar was. Everyone in town did. The man was a legend, one of the most influential corporate consultants in the world. In fact, as Tess understood it, he'd had something to do with helping the founders of Rachel's get their business off the ground.

Pindar was Sofia's *husband*?

Tess looked at Dee again. "The Pindar Principle?"

"*The more you give, the more you have*. Pindar teaches something he calls the Five Laws of Stratospheric Success . . ."

Tess knew about Pindar's Five Laws, too—everyone who'd ever worked at Rachel's did.

". . . and that's where the 5 Secrets originally came from," Dee was saying. "At least that's what Sofia says. Although Pindar swears it's the other way around. But then, they each claim they owe their career's success to the other one. And each is adamant that they're the one who married up. Ach, those two!"

She chuckled.

"Now, there is one stratospherically healthy ecology."

As Dee drove away, Tess checked the time. Jamie's school session wasn't quite over yet. For the next ten minutes, she sat in her car, sorting through her feelings and revelations. There was a lot to sort.

Where to start?

It was undeniable that for the past few years, she'd come to feel like she was suffocating; and she'd been blaming Tom for it; and she'd been feeling guilty about all of the above. How had Dee put it? *Marriage can be quite the puzzle.*

Although it seemed to Tess it was not marriage but she herself who was the puzzle here.

Actually, more of a tangled knot than a puzzle. And she was starting to see how to untangle it.

You want to heal a marriage? Feed the soil.

First off, she needed to stop blaming Tom for how she was feeling—and stop blaming herself, too. Just let all that go. That was the Third Secret, right? *Allow.* And didn't that mean to be *allowing* with yourself, too?

To fully love another, you have to fully love yourself.

Then, she needed to *do* something. To unsuffocate. She needed to find some way to put her problem-solving skills to work again. To stretch herself.

To grow.

Great—but how? She loved Jamie with all her heart, and she would not do anything to compromise his care and upbringing, which made this an irreconcilable conflict. There had to be a solution . . . but if there was, Tess wasn't seeing it.

She took a deep breath. *Trust*, she told herself.

When you're truly on each other's team, there is nothing the world can throw at you that you cannot handle.

It wasn't until she'd gone inside, extracted Jamie, gotten him snugly buckled in, and settled herself back into the driver's seat that it occurred to her—

That knot in her stomach.

It was gone.

The Fifth Secret
GROW

Every day, identify what you need to be happy, healthy, and fulfilled—and then give yourself that. Dare to dream a bigger dream for yourself.

12. Jeremiah

Jeremiah reached into a vest pocket and withdrew a thin silver pocket watch.

"Well, young man. You should be moving on to your next appointment."

Tom blinked. He was so engrossed in Mr. Janell's fable and his own reflections that he had nearly forgotten why he was there. It was time for his final interview with the CEO! Yet rather than getting to his feet, Tom stayed seated, looking at his sketch of that little cathedral and its dazzling stained-glass window.

Finally, he looked up.

"Sir?" he said. "Jeremiah? Can I ask *you* a question? I mean, a personal question."

Jeremiah cocked his head and peered at Tom, bemused. "Please."

"Why are you retiring?"

"Ah," said Jeremiah. "That *is* personal." He looked up at the ceiling for a moment, then back at Tom. "What do the rumors say?"

Tom felt himself blush. Jeremiah was right, of course; there had been rumors. That the old man couldn't keep up with the job. That he was getting a little . . . *quirky* was the euphemism Tom had heard.

"I don't listen to rumors," Tom replied.

Jeremiah nodded with approval. "Diplomatically put." He stood, turned ninety degrees, and began pacing along the wall of floor-to-ceiling glass.

"I was married, you know. For many, many magnificent years. Of which, I will add, every moment was a jewel that I keep even now, in my heart of hearts."

Tom practically held his breath. Mr. Janell was known to be an intensely private person, but even so, it startled him that he'd never heard even the slightest hint of there ever being a Mrs. Janell.

"There were, alas, health complications," Jeremiah continued.

"I'm so sorry," Tom mumbled.

"Not at all," said Jeremiah. "Actually, thank you for asking your question. It's good to talk about her." He paused his pacing. "You are a lucky man, Tom." He sighed, then resumed his slow pacing.

"All my life, mountain climbing was my passion. I traveled far and wide to find new cliffs to scale. When Lily's condition worsened, I put a halt to my expeditions and stayed home so that I could look after her.

"The illness progressed, slowly but persistently.

"And then, eventually, rather more quickly.

"Shall I tell you her last words to me? 'Remy,' she said, 'love of my life? Promise me something.' 'Anything,' I replied. And she said, 'Promise me you'll keep climbing. Promise me. And when you arrive at the summit, I'll be there.'"

His smile was distant, wistful. "She wanted my happiness, even more than I did. No." He frowned. "That's not quite right.

Let's say it this way: My happiness *was* her happiness." Again, that wistful smile. "And hers," he added softly, "was mine."

Jeremiah came to a stop directly in front of the photo of that mountaintop scene and gazed at it as he continued speaking.

"At any rate, I kept my promise. There are seven great peaks in the world that I had always wanted to summit. This," he nodded at the photo, "was number six. Just about a year ago. When I arrived back at base camp, I decided it was high time to hand over the reins here and go climb number seven."

He turned and looked at Tom. "And that is why old Mr. Janell is retiring. Old Mr. Janell has an appointment at twenty thousand feet."

He glanced at his timepiece again. "Nearly time. I'll leave you to it, then." He abruptly strode over to where Tom sat and jutted out his hand. "Do yourself proud in there."

Tom stood and shook Jeremiah's hand. He started to say "thank you," but the older man spoke up again.

"Tom." He put his other hand over Tom's and held it in his grip. "Some people build cathedrals; some climb mountains; some tell stories. Don't wait until you're seventy."

"No, sir. And . . . thank you."

As he reached the door, Tom had a thought and turned back. "Sir? I have to know. What were the leaves saying?"

Jeremiah looked puzzled. "Leaves?"

"In the story," said Tom. "The susurrus. You said susurrus was the language of love—but what was it *saying*?"

Jeremiah gave a slow blink.

"Ah," he said. "The whispering of the leaves."

He paused and let out a deep sigh.

"In my years here at Rachel's Famous Coffee, I have told this little story of the young couple and the tree fifty-seven times." He nodded in Tom's direction. "Fifty-eight now. And you are the first, the very first, to ask me that question." He turned and looked out through the plate-glass window. "The wind, the leaves, the tree . . . What were they saying?"

As Jeremiah looked back at Tom, his face slowly lit up, until he was beaming like a child.

"They were saying, *Thank you.* In ten thousand different ways, with ten thousand voices, yet all whispering the same refrain—

"Thank you . . .

"Thank you . . .

"Thank you . . ."

Tom stepped out of the office that felt like a mountaintop aerie and pulled the door shut behind him. It closed with a whisper.

Thank you, he thought. *Thank you.*

He walked down the hall and entered the office of the assistant to the CEO, with whom he would be having his second and final hour-long interview of the day.

The assistant, a young man who seemed to Tom barely older than Jamie, glanced up. "Tom, right?"

Tom nodded.

"She should be just another few minutes. You okay to wait?"

Tom smiled.

"Of course," he said. He was more than okay.

By the end of our interview, you'll know whether you're the right person for the job.

That was one of the very first things Jeremiah had said, at the start of their interview. And he was right, of course. Tom hadn't known whether he was the right person for the position when he first sat down in that office. He'd thought he knew, but he didn't.

He did now.

13. The Choice

When Tom arrived home late that afternoon, he found Tess sitting alone in the kitchen, chewing on a fingernail. Jamie was at a playdate down the street, something Tess had set up specifically so that she and Tom would have a little pocket of time alone together to process the news. Whether good or bad.

She left off torturing her poor fingernail and placed both hands on the kitchen table as Tom slowly pulled out a chair and sat down next to her.

"Well?" she said. "How goes it in the kingdom?"

Tom looked at her. "That Mr. Janell," he said, "is one odd duck." He thought for a moment, then laughed. "Or odd owl, I suppose."

Tess took a breath to keep from screaming, *Tell me! Tell me!* "Odd, how?"

"At the start of the interview, he said the strangest thing. He said by the end of the hour, I would know if I was the right person for the job."

"Okay . . ."

"Not *he* would know. *I* would know. I remember thinking, *Isn't that backward?*"

He went silent for a moment.

"Tom," said Tess. "I'm dying over here. So what happened?"

"Well . . . they offered me the job."

A flood of relief washed over her, and she sank back in her chair. "Oh, Tom! That's wonderful!" She jumped up and hugged him, then pulled back, still holding his shoulders with both hands, and looked into his face, her own face beaming like a lighthouse. "And I'm not the least bit surprised, either—I *knew* they would do this. You so deserve this, Tom. You do!"

"Yes," Tom agreed, "apparently I do. But I turned it down."

"Ha, ha. Not funny, mister." She sat back down again.

He didn't reply.

"What," said Tess, and she felt suddenly chilled. "I don't get it. What's the joke?"

"Well," he said, "I told them I was honored, of course. And incredibly grateful. But that in all honesty, I thought another candidate would be a better fit for the job. And after a good, long talk, they agreed."

Tess stared at him.

"I don't understand. You're serious? They handed you the position—the position you've been dying to get, your dream job—and you told them to give it *to someone else instead*?"

He nodded. "That's pretty much how it went, yes."

"I don't . . . Why would you . . . ? Tom, are you *nuts*?"

Tom smiled. "Probably. Don't you want to know who I suggested?"

"What? No! Who?"

"You."

"*Me?*"

Tom leaned forward and kissed her, then took her by the shoulders and looked her in the eyes, just as she'd done moments earlier.

"I am absolutely, one hundred percent serious. I told them you were the very best person on earth for this job. Because you are. And they were inclined to agree. Mr. Janell even said it: they've missed you."

She gawped at him, struggling to find words to fit her confusion.

"You've got a series of interviews scheduled for tomorrow morning," Tom added. "If you want them."

"But . . ." She looked around the kitchen, as if trying to picture what he was saying. "But who'll look after Jamie?"

"I will, of course."

"*You?* Tom, you'll go crazy!"

"A chance to spend time with my son?" He smiled and shook his head. "I don't think so. But if I do, it'll be a good kind of crazy."

Tess couldn't stop staring at him as it started to sink in. Her . . . back at Rachel's? "They'd never give me that position."

"They've booked you for tomorrow morning at nine. If you say yes, that is."

"But I haven't been there for years! I'd be practically starting out all over again. We can't afford the drop in pay."

"No drop. They'd be offering you the same salary they were offering me."

"But . . . I can't just pick up and go. I can't abandon our family. Jamie needs me!"

"Yes," said Tom. "Jamie needs you, and I need you. Most of all, *you* need you. And this *is* you, Tess. You're brilliant at this stuff. You know you are. This is what you were born to do."

"Tom, this is your dream job. I can't let you give that up."

He smiled. "I think I'm actually gaining a lot more than I'm giving up."

Tess shook her head, still trying to fully grasp this new reality. "How will you manage?"

He took both her hands in his.

"We'll get up in the morning. I'll make you a cup of hot coffee, first thing. Send you off. Then go watch our son build his life." He smiled. "Maybe, in the little stretches and odd moments when he doesn't need me, I'll doodle."

Maybe, he thought, those doodles would grow into something.

Maybe something like the next *Little Prince*.

14. Tessandtom

The aroma reached her nostrils even before she opened the front door. She stopped and took a slow inhale, savoring the scent, then opened the door and went inside.

She slipped off her jacket and hung it on a hook in the hallway, then stood still again, listening, relishing the moment of quiet anticipation. It was one of her favorite parts of the day.

She proceeded down the hall, the aroma growing stronger as she approached the kitchen. Dinner was simmering on the stove, and nearly ready by the smell of it.

She bent over the big pan, closed her eyes, and took another long inhale of saffron and rosemary. He had just about mastered Sofia's recipe. Her new favorite.

Heaven on a spoon.

She opened her eyes and noticed the cardboard carton sitting on the kitchen table, stenciled labeling on the side facing her:

CASE OF 24

AUTHOR'S COPIES

The top of the carton had been slit open, the topmost of its two dozen volumes removed.

She heard the sound of laughter drifting down from upstairs.

She approached the table. There was a card by her place setting, along with a little wrapped box. The inscription on the envelope said, "Happy Second Anniversary, Ms. COO." She picked up the card and smiled. She would wait to open it and the little wrapped box until they were all seated here together.

Happy second anniversary.

Was it really two years already? It seemed like it had been two weeks, or maybe two days. The blink of an eye. Two years of gazing out at those magnificent western mountains as she talked on her phone or videoconferenced at her desk; two years of grappling with the complexities involved in steering and managing a global enterprise that touched the lives of millions.

And she'd loved it. Loved every last insanely challenging, maddeningly crazy moment of it.

Still, this, right now, was her favorite part. Coming home every day was the saffron on her paella.

She set the envelope down and left the kitchen, following the voices like a trail of magic breadcrumbs.

She found the two of them upstairs, Tom stretched out on Jamie's bed, Jamie curled up against him, both holding the book as Tom read aloud. From her spot, peeking in through the bedroom door, Tess could just see the embossed gold-foil Caldecott sticker, and above it the glossy hardcover's title:

The Boy Who Talked to the Wind

"Room for one more?" she said.

Jamie looked up, his eyes wide with excitement. "Mom! Did you know Dad *wrote* this?!"

She nodded. "So I heard."

"So, you are not gonna *believe* this! So there's this boy, who lives in a little village at the foot of this wise old mountain, and he's out one morning walking his dog, and his dog gets loose and starts trotting up the street, and the boy follows him all the way to the edge of the village and up onto the mountain, and he goes up this mountain path for like *hours*, and then he comes to this flat part all covered with trees and stands there listening to the wind in the leaves, and then the wind—Mom, *it says his name!*"

"Whoa," said Tess.

The boy turned to his father and said, "So what does he *do*? What happens next?"

Tom glanced at his watch. "I don't know, buddy, supper's just about ready. Maybe we should go eat."

"Pleeeease? Just one more chapter?"

Tom looked up at Tess, her sandy hair haloed by the bright hallway light behind her. "Your call, Mama. You wanna hear what happens next?"

She smiled, then crawled over onto the far side of the bed and curled up against him, her head nestled onto his shoulder as she imagined the sound of the wind in the leaves.

"Tell me more," she said.

The 5 Secrets to Lasting Love

APPRECIATE. Look for specific things about your partner that you love, and when you notice them, take a moment to tell them.

ATTEND. Convey your love through some meaningful, tangible action. Pay attention. Notice what your partner needs, wants, and loves, then give them that.

ALLOW. Take responsibility for the energy you bring to the relationship. Accept your partner for who they are, the way they are. Be their safe harbor. Have a generous spirit. Be kind.

BELIEVE. Believe in your partner wholeheartedly. Give them your complete, unshakable trust. Let your faith show.

GROW. Every day, identify what you need to be happy, healthy, and fulfilled—and then give yourself that. Dare to dream a bigger dream for yourself.

The Practice

Love Is a Practice

When the original *Go-Giver* came out in 2008, it struck a chord throughout the business community. From mom-and-pops to multinationals, entrepreneurs to chambers of commerce, people began using the book to define a new values-based way of doing business in the twenty-first century.

But something else happened that we didn't quite foresee. People started telling us they were using *The Go-Giver* not only in their businesses but also in their schools, churches, communities, and homes.

Even in their marriages.

And they started asking, "When will you write a *Go-Giver* book about building successful relationships?"

At the same time, for years friends had been asking the two of us, what was our secret? What kept our love so fresh and alive? We'd both been through plenty of hardships, both in our own lives and in our lives together. Yet through it all, our love and happiness only grew stronger. As one friend put it, "What's your secret sauce?"

We gave that question quite a bit of thought, and eventually we both arrived at the same conclusion. Our secret sauce came down to one word: *giving*. We both approached our marriage with a spirit of generosity. Our own marriage, and all the marriages of people we observed and talked with over those years that exhibited that same kind of enduring love—love that grows and deepens with time, rather than being diminished by the stresses of life—embodied what we've come to know as the Pindar Principle:

The more you give, the more you have.

That's where these 5 Secrets come from.

In the sections that follow, we'll look at each secret from three different points of view:

Why It Works: A brief explanation of some of the concepts underlying each secret, in terms of our childhood development and maturation.

What It Looks Like: A picture of how this secret actually plays out in our day-to-day lives and behavior, with a few examples from the lives of friends and clients we've known.

Your Daily Practice: A simple formula for how to put each of the 5 Secrets into practice every day.

You've probably heard the expression "Practice makes perfect." We don't think this is true. Becoming perfect would mean there'd be no more room to improve and grow. In our experience, practice does not make you perfect—but it does make you better.

This is true for anything you do. It's true for dancing, painting, carpentry, and baseball. For teaching, parenting, and coaching. It's true for the practice of prayer and the practice of meditation.

And it's true for lasting love.

It might not seem like love should be something you practice at—yet it is. Love can be a bolt from the blue, something that wallops you at first sight (as it did for Tom and Tess), or it can blossom over time from a friendship. But whatever form love takes, love that endures—lasting love—is a practice.

This practice does not make your love perfect, but it does make your love better: deeper, richer, more satisfying, more uplifting. It strengthens your bond, fortifies your capacity to hold each other up and be each other's safe harbor in good times and bad.

And it is, absolutely, a practice.

Meaningful change doesn't happen "someday." It happens today, right now. To bring these secrets to life as an active, positive force in your relationship, make them something you *do*, consciously and intentionally.

Keep it simple. Lasting love is like good health: more than any grand gestures or big, dramatic life changes, it's built out of the little things you do every day.

Sometimes the smallest things make the biggest difference— especially when you do them consistently.

Appreciate

Look for specific things about your partner that you love,
and when you notice them, take a moment to tell them.

Why It Works

Being appreciated reaches back to the roots of our earliest experiences in life. It touches that place psychologists call "primary narcissism," which begins in an infant's desire to be admired, talked to, and cooed over.

This need to be witnessed, understood, and loved is our oldest and most primary bonding ritual, which is why it has such power in our lives. It never leaves us.

Even as adults, it's impossible to overstate how deeply we long to be witnessed.

Yet we often overlook this, both for ourselves and for the people we love. Opportunities to witness our partner through the simple expression of appreciation fly past us constantly, yet we easily fail to notice them. The fast-moving train of our life leads us to focus on our own personal reality.

As much as we love each other, we can start to feel we are moving through life unnoticed, invisible, and alone.

And yet the entire tone of our relationships can shift by simply taking a few moments each day to witness the people closest to us.

What It Looks Like

In coaching appreciation, we often start with inviting our client to talk about the things they love about their spouse, which often leads to early stories of the couple's courtship and what it was that first drew them together.

This is a great place to start.

Your first objective is to make a list of as many things you love and appreciate about your partner as you can come up with. We like to make that list as long as possible. It's like a treasure hunt, and the more questions you ask yourself, the more treasures you'll find.

At first, this may take some careful thought. Like Nicole in the story, you may even freeze up. That's okay. It's like using a muscle you haven't exercised in a while. Don't worry if it takes you real effort to nail down something specific. And even if, as with Nicole, it feels a little awkward or forced, persevere. It will soon feel more natural. In time, you'll find these things come to you spontaneously, out of the blue.

One man told us he loved what a good cook his wife was. Just like Nicole, who thought and thought and finally blurted out,

"He makes a wicked lasagna," he said it was the only thing he could think of in the moment.

We asked him to say more about that.

"Well," he said after thinking for a moment, "I never really liked salad. But all my life, the only salads I ever had were made with store-bought dressings. Karen never buys bottled dressing. She makes her dressings fresh, with a bunch of different ingredients, I'm not even sure what, but they're delicious, and after eight years of living together, I've realized I *love* salad."

And then he looked at us and voiced that thing that so many people think: "That's kind of silly, isn't it? I mean, salad? Does that even count?"

No! It's not silly at all. And yes! It totally counts. It's real. It's authentic.

Sure, it's a little thing—but it's a little thing with big meaning.

The qualities and actions you find to notice and appreciate don't have to be deep insights. "I love your smile." "Thank you so much for the way you take out the trash every week." "I *loved* that salad you made!" These are all expressions of love as valid and eloquent as any Shakespearean sonnet.

In order to appreciate someone, you first have to pay attention to what in particular you love about that person. It's such a simple action, but one we often don't take time to do. Once you make the decision to pay attention, you'll find there are so many moments every day when your partner shows their warm and vulnerable side, or their sense of humor, their tenderness in talking to your child, or their patience when the house is in chaos and you've spent the entire day with a sick child or a newborn baby and there's no dinner in sight.

Sometimes we appreciate each other in odd moments when the stress is high and our partner lightens our load in some appreciable way. It can be a simple touch, a gift of a favorite dinner during a hard workweek, or a chance to take a hot bath when you've been home all day with a rambunctious toddler and you're simply exhausted.

The most important part of this secret is taking the moment to stop your partner and *tell them* exactly what it is you appreciate about them.

Appreciation can become a new way of saying, "I love you." It can also become a new way of flirting.

One woman told us she had a fun moment with appreciating her husband in a playful way by saying, "Hey, have I told you yet today that you have the best-looking butt in blue jeans?" The shock on his face was followed by a big grin. "Yeah? Well, it's even cuter out of blue jeans!" to which she replied, "Consider that a date, buddy."

He then left for Little League practice with a car full of kids, and she went on with her day's activities—but that brief moment of flirting with active appreciation started everyone's day out with good feelings.

Appreciation has its familiar opposite, namely criticism.

The truly toxic thing about criticism is that it easily becomes a self-perpetuating cycle. Criticism creates its own momentum. The more you allow yourself to be irritated, the more you find to be irritated about. Criticism snowballs. It's like picking at a loose thread on a sweater—before you know it, the whole thing has come unraveled.

So what do you do? Every time you notice you're keeping score or mentally picking on some behavior, stop, take a breath, and ask yourself, "What am I grateful for about this person?" Put the First Secret into practice, then and there: find something you love about your partner, and tell them.

It's just as easy to find things to appreciate as it is to find things to criticize. As Nicole tells Tess, "It's purely a question of where you put your focus. And what you focus on increases. All it takes is a decision, and it's a choice you make over and over."

As you do, you'll find that appreciation, too, creates its own momentum. The more you voice your appreciation, the more you'll discover to appreciate.

Your Daily Practice

Each day, find three things to appreciate about your partner, and take the time to tell them.

Start with just once a day. Notice one thing your partner does that you appreciate, and point it out to them. Compliment them for it. Thank them for it.

Do that today. Then do it again tomorrow. And the next day.

When it feels comfortable, turn up the volume: Take it up to two times a day. Then three. Keep each appreciation simple and authentic.

The ground rules are simple: keep it real, specific, and spoken.

Real: This needs to be an authentic compliment or statement of appreciation that your spouse will receive as genuine and real.

Specific: Praise and acknowledgment are far more powerful when they are quite specific. "You're a great person" isn't nearly as meaningful as "You're so thoughtful—I love how you're always looking out for other people's feelings."

Spoken: This is key! We often appreciate things in other people without ever giving that appreciation a voice. It's nice that you think your partner is attractive, but if you keep it to yourself, you're the only one who benefits from that warm, fuzzy feeling. Share it!

Doing this consistently sets a new tone in the relationship. These expressions of appreciation will often bring both of you, giver and receiver, spontaneous feelings of warmth and affection.

Remember that one of our deepest longings is the desire to be witnessed.

People often ask, "Does this need to be something new every day?" Not necessarily. Sometimes you'll naturally repeat something you've said or done before, and this can have a very meaningful power of its own. It never gets old to say, "I love your smile."

To fulfill the practice, though, the words or gestures need to *feel* brand-new, which simply means they need to be real and authentic in the moment. You don't want to slide into something that feels rote, routine, or like "going through the motions." Making the effort to find something genuinely new and different to appreciate is a great way to expand and deepen your love for each other.

It can be helpful to keep a journal as you go. Writing down each new appreciation can help it stick, and it's fun to go back and see what you said two weeks ago, or six months ago. You'll be amazed at what you come up with over time.

Examples of Appreciation

There is no appreciation too basic or too simple to be worth expressing. Sometimes all it takes is a sincere "thank you." You might sincerely appreciate your partner:

- for their thoughtfulness, kindness, patience, insight, honesty, or sense of humor.
- for being a generous person and always giving people the benefit of the doubt.
- for their parenting in any situation, from taking the kids Christmas shopping, to dealing with a tantrum, to taking care of a sick child in the night.
- for their physical appearance (in and out of clothing).

- for chores done (and forget the scorecard on the ones that are not!).
- for buying you a special gift you thought they didn't know you wanted.
- for helping with dinner or making breakfast.
- for their encouragement, support, and kind words just when you needed them.
- for bragging to a friend about your recent accomplishment at work.
- for smiling at you when you wake up and kissing you before bed.
- for making time for sex and keeping it in the schedule.
- for being a steady and constant breadwinner.
- for being smart—who doesn't want to be told they're smart and appreciated for it?
- for picking up the miles of toys that toddlers leave all over the house daily.
- for tracking and paying the bills, doing the taxes, or keeping track of all the kids' dental and medical appointments.
- for leaving you love notes or sending flirtatious text messages.
- for being a good parent—there can never be too much praise and appreciation for this!

Attend

Convey your love through some meaningful, tangible action. Pay attention. Notice what your partner needs, wants, and loves, then give them that.

Why It Works

Like being appreciated, being attended to has its roots in our early childhood. Being fed by a spoon in a highchair is being attended to. Being held when you cry is being attended to. At that stage of development, our very life depends on someone close to us taking the time, multiple times a day, to feed us, bathe us, diaper us, comfort us, and take care of all our needs.

As we grow and develop, we gain an increasing amount of autonomy; with each new chapter in our lives, we more clearly establish our independence. We no longer need to be fed, or bathed, or clothed. We run our own checking accounts, drive our own cars, and manage our own careers.

Yet the child at our core never leaves us. We still remember these simple acts of love and the people behind them—the grandmother who knitted us a sweater in our favorite color, or the mom who made our favorite cake for our birthday simply because she knew it was our favorite. We remember the parent who held us as infants when we needed to be held; who rubbed our back when we were upset by something mean a classmate said to us, who told us it wasn't true and reminded us that we were good and kind; who made us a cup of hot cocoa on a cold, lonely day to cheer us up.

What It Looks Like

We often practice the Second Secret spontaneously and instinctively when we're first dating, showering each other with gifts, holding hands on dinner dates, and finding little ways to show our affection.

Over time, though, as we start building our lives together, things get a little more complicated. It can take some careful attention to sleuth out exactly what each of us truly needs in order to feel well attended to.

Our fondest childhood memories may involve cakes and cocoa; as grown-ups, it's not always quite that simple. Adults have adult needs, wants, and interests.

A woman we know had a habit of putting little love notes in her children's lunch boxes before sending them off to school. One day she decided to start sending them to her husband as well—not on slips of paper in a lunch box but as text messages at various moments of the day. She started by texting him brief words of appreciation and praise; soon she added in a scattering of steamy love notes.

This had a profound effect on her husband. He admitted that he had missed the sense of romance and adventure in their lives, and that he had begun to worry that he was becoming a boring person.

"I definitely do not feel boring anymore!" he told us. They both laughed when they told us what had happened, sheepishly admitting that this simple thing had become a new way of flirting and creating intimacy in their lives.

"It's kind of outrageous," said the woman. "After three kids and fourteen years of marriage, our intimate life has become way more personal and satisfying."

All because one person started attending to her partner in a new and creative way.

Just as the First Secret has its opposite, so does the second. The opposite of attending is neglecting.

Feeling ignored can be soul-crushing and can have a deep impact on a marriage. The opposite of love is not hate but ambivalence. Yet neglect often occurs unconsciously, without malice or intention. Time goes by; life happens. We each get overloaded with the stresses of our own lives. Without meaning to, we start letting our attention slide. We take our partner for granted. We coast.

Owen and Kate had been married for six years and had two toddlers under the age of three. Owen had a high-stress job and arrived home every day to find Kate feeling worn out from her long day with the kids, and the house in a state of chaos—toys scattered everywhere, abandoned snacks on tables, and a general mess. The kids needed baths and were already hungry, but Kate didn't feel she could start in on those tasks until Owen arrived and either watched the kids or helped with dinner.

This made Owen feel secretly grumpy. All he wanted was a little time to relax and unwind, and while he dearly loved his children, the chaos of the house felt overwhelming. He knew Kate was a great mom who gave their two toddlers her undivided attention all day long, and that what she needed when he got home was a little time to regroup and regain her sense of self—but he was immobilized by his own sense of being overwhelmed.

It also made Kate feel terrible. She could look past the general mess, but she was desperate for some time to herself to take an uninterrupted bath, or a jog, or both.

Owen wanted less mess and more order. Kate simply wanted to escape.

It would have been so easy for the two to start blaming each other, letting the minor irritations turn over time into deep-set grievances. This is how the bond of marriage is so often eroded: each person feeling the pain of their own unmet needs yet not seeing the unmet needs of the other.

When Kate and Owen sat down one evening and honestly opened up about how they felt at the end of the day, they realized they were equally frazzled by the situation—and equally overwhelmed by their growing frustration over what to do about it.

They each became aware of the other's perspective.

They paid attention.

The question suddenly became a cooperative venture: How could they each help take care of the other's needs without going nuts with their own unmet needs?

Kate acknowledged that she'd always been messier than Owen, and she knew that disorder threw him off. Even in college, he couldn't study, focus, or relax if his room wasn't clean. He described himself as "needing a little Zen in his life."

So Kate decided to make the effort to ensure that all the scattered toys were completely picked up before Owen arrived home. She stocked every room with toy boxes and baskets so she could quickly skip from room to room picking up—she even got their toddlers to join in. She loaded all the dishes into the dishwasher and wiped down all the counters so the general appearance of the house was clean and organized. To her surprise, it took her only fifteen minutes to conquer the chaos.

She also made sure to feed the children ahead of Owen's arrival, so they would be less hungry and out of sorts.

When Owen arrived, the complete shift in the state of their home was a more-than-pleasant surprise. After a few days of playing with his sons and enjoying his newfound sense of relaxation after work, he suggested that he take the boys for an hour while Kate took a jog and a bath before dinner.

Kate was so elated that she soon began to prep dinner in advance so it could be in the oven while she was jogging and bathing.

Owen got his after-work relaxation time—his "little bit of Zen."

Kate got her uninterrupted jog and bath.

The kids got to eat early, enjoy a little relaxed time with their dad, and have a mom who was a whole lot less frazzled.

This was more than a simple matter of task allocation. This was a major triumph for their marriage. It meant they each needed to take a step back from their own growing frustration and see the situation from the other's point of view. They each needed, in other words, to view their mutual challenge from the standpoint not of *getting* what they felt they needed, but of *giving* what the other person needed.

And it transformed their marriage.

As time went on, Owen started bathing the boys while Kate jogged, which took even more stress off their evening routine, which in turn allowed bedtime to occur a little earlier, giving them more time to be a couple once the kids were asleep. They began to enjoy quiet candlelight dinners alone at eight, instead of stressed, hurried meals at six thirty when they were both still exhausted from their days.

At those dinners, the conversations roamed far and wide. They learned more about each other in those dinnertime chats than they had in years. Their friendship deepened, and with it, their love.

Your Daily Practice

> Find at least one way each day to show your love for your partner through some meaningful, tangible action.

Pay attention to the things that matter to your partner. Observe the things that make them feel loved and comforted.

You may want to start an actual list, writing down what you know about your partner and what you learn as you pay attention. What is their favorite color? Flavor? Favorite foods? Favorite music, band, movie, book? What are some of their favorite ways to relax and unwind? If they had an hour free, just to themselves, what would they do with it?

You can take this further by interviewing your partner. Ask them about the special moments they remember most from their childhood, the memories they treasure.

Each individual's sensory and emotional patterns have deep roots in their early childhood; the things that make one feel comforted and attended to are distinct and specific. As Jeremiah puts it, each relationship is as unique as a fingerprint.

Attending may sometimes take the form of a gift, but it's important to understand that a gift's value is determined not by how much it cost, or how useful it is, or how much *you* like it, but by the thoughtfulness of the choice. What it is matters far less than what it means to your partner.

It means you were paying attention. You cared enough to make the effort.

To attend is to be *attuned*. Tune to your partner's channel. Put yourself in their shoes. Practice empathy.

Sometimes the greatest gift in the moment is to simply listen without judgment or commentary. It can be tempting to want to rush in and respond, to give advice, to solve the problem. Resist that urge. The point of listening is not to "fix" anything but to be there, hearing, accepting, understanding, and learning.

Being heard has tremendous power; in a marriage, it opens communication in myriad ways.

Often the most meaningful gifts are the simple gestures and actions that respond to your partner's needs in ways that build their sense of being witnessed, understood, and cared for. In the story of the young man and the princess, the young man noticed his wife's love of cinnamon (although she'd never mentioned it) and brought her cinnamon tea in bed, which made her feel valued and cared for. She noticed that his shoulders were sore after a long day of construction work and gave him a shoulder and neck massage.

Both of them felt taken care of and attended to by the other. Both of them received it as love, and their little tree flourished.

Examples of Attending

There are ten thousand ways you can find to convey your care and thoughtfulness to your partner. You might attend to their needs and wants by:

- remembering their favorite foods, snacks, drinks, colors, or flowers.
- showing affection; reaching out and touching their hand, giving a hug.
- doing the laundry or other chores you don't normally take on.

- remembering not only their birthday but also their parents' birthdays and any other dates that are important to them. (Note: calendars!)
- noticing when they're blue, or upset about something; asking if they're okay; and then genuinely listening to their answer (just listening, not trying to process or fix).
- rubbing their aching shoulders or feet, or drawing them a hot bath before bed.
- bringing them hot tea or coffee in bed in the morning or pouring them a glass of wine or their favorite mocktail after work; bringing them an unexpected snack when you know they're working extra hard.
- baking (or buying at the bakery) their favorite oatmeal raisin cookies or cinnamon coffee cake out of the blue, just because you know it's their favorite.

Allow

Take responsibility for the energy you bring to the relationship.
Accept your partner for who they are, the way they are.
Be their safe harbor. Have a generous spirit. Be kind.

Why It Works

As we grow through childhood and into our teens, we step out of primary narcissism and learn to accommodate our own needs to those of the people around us.

This is not always easy. As an infant, the world was your domain. It all revolved around you. Now there are other people entering your bubble. This can be fun and exciting and wonderful—but it can also be fraught with friction and discomfort.

As adults, we each still live within that bubble that defines who we are. When two of us come together to form a long-term, committed relationship, we are each letting the other person into our bubble. A new space opens up: the intersection of our two spheres. We each bring our own energy to that new space.

This new space defines the *us*.

This is the essence of marriage: we each maintain our integrity as our own individual selves, yet in our intersection we also create a third, entirely new space between us with a life and quality of its own—the energy of the marriage itself. The *us*.

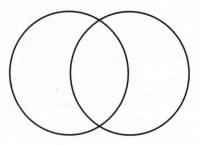

Here is the challenge: How do two fully grown, complex personalities, each with their own unique family histories, occupy the same space?

By allowing.

Allowing means taking responsibility for the energy you bring to your marriage—and giving your partner the space to do the same.

What It Looks Like

When we first fall in love, it can be incredibly easy to share this new space. The flush of new romance casts a rosy glow over everything. We adore every little thing about the other person. We're crazy about each other!

What could go wrong?

But we are all shaped by our family histories and past relationships—and we bring those histories with us. In time, patterns emerge that reflect those unresolved emotional experiences.

This can lead one or both of you to start making your love conditional: "I love you—except when you act like that." "I love you—but I love you more when you behave this way, and not that way." In other words, not allowing your partner to be their authentic self.

Another way of *not allowing* is to deny, actively resist, or try to control the other person's needs and feelings. This, too, often happens without malice or conscious intention, but it can be terribly destructive.

Sarah and James had a problem in their marriage. Sarah had been assaulted while in college and had residual post-traumatic anxiety that she'd addressed with both therapy and medication. Yet despite her best efforts, she still had a tendency to be anxious or nervous about new situations—and in those moments, her anxiety would make James uncomfortable.

James would express this by telling Sarah to relax. "Calm down," he'd say. "Stop worrying." His tone was, by his own admission, not reassuring or comforting. He felt that her anxiety was something she could control if she tried, and that after so much therapy she should be better able to manage it.

James's response to her anxiety made Sarah feel criticized, hurt, and dismissed, which only made her anxiety grow. Now she felt the need to mask her authentic responses to situations that made her nervous.

This became the elephant in the room between them. James would occasionally say things like "There you go again. Just let go, it's not a big deal!" In response, Sarah would go to their bedroom and cry.

The real problem was that James wasn't allowing the space for Sarah's anxiety to exist, let alone to heal or even be witnessed without criticism.

The opposite of allowing is controlling. This is what James was trying to do.

This is not to cast James as the bad guy here. James, too, was acting out of his own history with trauma. His father, a Vietnam veteran who had spent years self-medicating with alcohol, had modeled for James a pattern of denial in the face of discomfort that made him feel helpless to respond to Sarah's anxiety in a supportive way. Instead, his reflexive response was to try to make it go away. By denying her experience ("It's no big deal!"), he was distancing himself from the problem and making it her fault.

A psychologist might call this "a pattern of codependent coercion." You could also call it *not allowing*. By not allowing Sarah to feel the way she felt, James was pushing her out of that space between them, the space that was their relationship.

Whenever one member of a couple is not conscious of the energy they bring to the relationship, that space between them gets filled by old, unresolved issues, relationships, and unconscious communication patterns, often leading to such negative responses as criticism, denial, control, codependence, and the whole gamut of dysfunctional behaviors.

As James began learning about the 5 Secrets, he found himself stumbling over secret number three. The idea of "allowing" made him feel anxious and out of control. When asked what energy he wanted to hold between them, James broke down and cried. He realized that not being able to fix Sarah's anxiety made him feel completely helpless—and that trying to control Sarah's feelings was undermining their relationship.

In the months that followed, James made it his mission to bring a compassionate response to Sarah's feelings.

Sarah made her own effort, too: she made sure James knew how much she appreciated it whenever he responded that way.

They had a breakthrough one day when James blurted out, "Your anxiety makes me feel anxious!" and they both had a good laugh at the irony of it. Yet behind the laughter was an incredibly valuable insight: it was really James's own anxiety, not Sarah's, that was making him so uncomfortable. He was projecting his own issue onto her, making it her fault.

He hadn't been conscious of the energy he was bringing to their shared sphere.

As James continued to reflect and adopt a new pattern, Sarah did more work of her own. She also found a new compassion for the place in James that held his own history of trauma and felt anxious and out of control.

Anxiety became a place of joining for the couple, as they both saw the impact that feeling out of control had on each of them.

The Japanese have an art called *kintsugi*, meaning "to repair with gold," in which they put broken pieces of pottery back together by mending the breakage with lacquer laced with powdered precious metals. We believe a marriage can do much the same thing for us, only in this case, love is the gold that marks the lines of healing.

Rather than trying to hide or deny the broken places, the *kintsugi* artist honors and cherishes them.

This is what James and Sarah did.

Your Daily Practice

Find one new way each day to support your partner, give them the space they need, show kindness, or ease their burden.

In a way, allowing is more subtle than the first two secrets. It's easy to grasp what it means to appreciate someone and attend to their needs; we often do it instinctively the moment we start dating. Allowing, though, is something that typically shows up more over time.

The importance of allowing often becomes more obvious when times are tough than when all is smooth sailing. When the pressure is on, when there is stress or difficulty—that is precisely when we are most called upon to be allowing.

When under stress, it's easy to start drawing battle lines: to blame each other, find fault in the other. It's a natural, even primal response. Yet it's incredibly destructive. The moment you start drawing lines in the sand between the two of you—intentionally or not, aware of it or not—is the moment the *us* of your marriage starts to fracture.

Allowing means bringing a spirit of generosity to your marriage. Giving your partner support when they need it and giving them space when they need it. Protecting them when they need it. Running interference for them when they need it.

It means always giving your partner the benefit of the doubt and assuming they are acting with the best intentions. For example, if your partner is feeling irritable or snaps at you, allowing means responding with compassion, instead of taking it personally and lashing back at them.

Allowing means not making it about you.

Allowing also means throwing out the concept of a scorecard. ("Hey, I did the dishes every night last week, don't you think it's your turn?")

The power of allowing often comes more from what you *don't* do than what you do. You don't try to change the other person. You don't try to "fix" them, correct them, or "improve" them. In other words, you don't try to control who they are, how they feel, or how they behave.

Allowing is the "unconditional" part of unconditional love. When traditional marriage vows talk about loving each other "in sickness and in health," this is the "in sickness" part. You don't just love your partner when they're happy and healthy and buoyant—you also love them when they're having a rough time.

Examples of Allowing

Allowing is what you do when life is too big or too challenging for one person to take on alone. You might bring a generous spirit to your marriage by:

- taking over with the kids when your partner is at the end of their rope or just needs some time to themselves.
- handling a task or chore your partner normally manages when it's just too much, such as cleaning up the kitchen at night, vacuuming on the weekend, or doing an impromptu load of laundry.
- staying calm during an argument and being open to their point of view. (This is especially important in those moments when you're convinced that you're right!)
- dropping whatever you had planned in those moments when it feels important to your partner to do something different.
- letting go of defensive reactions and admitting when you are wrong, or forgot an important date, or messed up in some other way. Letting go of the ego's game of needing to be right.

Believe

Believe in your partner wholeheartedly. Give them your complete, unshakable trust. Let your faith show.

Why It Works

As grown adults, we may think we should be self-sufficient beings—but we each still have that vulnerable child inside who needs to be reminded who they are.

Some of us were fortunate enough to grow up with parents who believed in us, who praised us to the skies for taking that first little step and cheered us on even before we did it. "Look at you, reading that big word—I'll bet you can read that whole book yourself!"

For some, it was not necessarily our parents but a grandparent or favorite aunt, a teacher, that one high school coach, or even a best friend whose unshakable faith in us played a pivotal role in forming our sense of self.

This is still true today. Every one of us still needs someone close to us who believes in us.

We all have insecurities about who we are. Am I really capable? Am I really worthy? Attractive? A good person? Can I really do this? Will I ever achieve this thing I want to do? We're all asking these questions and harboring these self-doubts, even if it doesn't show on the outside.

When someone shows up who answers "Yes!" to all those questions, someone whose opinions matter to us, it has a profound impact. It becomes the energy that sustains us when we've lost a job, have suffered some other blow to our confidence, or are dealing with any sort of difficult transition.

That person—and more specifically that person's *belief in you*—becomes a critical power source. It's like plugging yourself into a wall socket: all your lights switch on and your battery starts to recharge.

What It Looks Like

It's easy for the stresses and challenges of everyday existence to pick away at our self-confidence. When life hurls sticks and stones at your partner, when they're struggling through a difficult situation or coping with a disappointment or failed effort, this is when they most need you standing next to them, reminding them of everything great about them.

This often means believing in your partner even when they don't believe in themselves. *Especially* when they don't believe in themselves.

This doesn't mean you think they're perfect or infallible. Of course they're flawed, just as we all are flawed. Unshakable faith in your partner means you believe in *the core of who they are.*

And what a difference it makes! Feeling your belief in them provides an enormous boost—like finding a sudden burst of renewed strength in the final lap of a long and arduous race. Experienced consistently over time, it generates a whole new level of energy and confidence.

Like appreciation, belief in our partner is something we can easily take for granted. We may believe in our partner but let that belief go unsaid for months or even years. Yet like appreciation, your belief in your partner is something that needs constant renewal. Make your faith visible. Share it. Express it. Communicate it. Doing so opens the door to a deeper intimacy. Communication improves, vulnerabilities get shared, and the obstacles couples face become points of joining rather than places to disengage.

Trust and communication go hand in hand. When you take away one, the other fades, too.

In the absence of open communication, we tend to make up our own story and project it onto the relationship. We start assuming what the other person thinks and feels, and that nagging critical inner voice most of us have can easily turn those assumptions toward the negative.

Trust is built on a foundation of belief. When we withhold our belief in each other, we steal from our bank of trust, often without realizing it. And the converse is true, too: when we openly communicate our trust, we build a surplus in that bank of trust that can carry us through even the most difficult times.

For example, two of the most common issues underlying marital conflict are sex and money. Not coincidentally, these are also two topics that couples often avoid talking about. Yet these are central dimensions in every marriage. Why would we shrink from talking openly and honestly about them?

In part, because these are deeply personal topics. Talking about either one can make us feel extremely vulnerable. Our comfort level here likely has roots in how such topics were handled in our family of origin. We may have inherited inhibitions or attitudes we need to overcome. Bottom line, though, it's an issue of trust—which is a reflection of our core belief in each other.

Elizabeth and Dan had been married for twenty-two years when Dan, who had been having some blood pressure issues, began to experience erectile dysfunction. At the time, Dan had recently been downsized from his sales management job of twenty years and was actively looking for a new job to carry them through to retirement. He was overweight and feeling the financial stress of his situation.

Elizabeth was also feeling the stress and knew they needed a change. Instead of making Dan feel bad that their sex life seemed stalled, she spent additional time sharing her faith in him—her faith that he could lose twenty pounds and take back his health, and her faith that he was an incredible guy with strong talents in his profession. One evening, as they were having an intimate conversation about all this, she let him know that she wanted their sex life to be warm and loving, not stressful, and that she thought a prescription for erectile dysfunction medication would make him not less of a man but more of one. She also let him know that he was the lover for her, that she still found him as attractive as ever and just wanted their sex life to be fun for him, too.

Elizabeth built their bank of trust by explicitly communicating her belief and faith in Dan.

In the months that followed, the couple made some powerful changes. With the aid of medication, their sex life returned and was more intimate than ever. Dan made some significant changes in his diet and began taking daily walks to get more exercise. Elizabeth soon joined him on the walks, and it became a time when they could break away from their teenage kids and have deeper talks about what was going on in their lives.

Dan poured a newfound energy into his online search for a new job and landed a position that was a step up the management ladder and gave him more perks and the opportunity to teach new sales professionals in his company. In every way, their lives entered a new chapter together.

Without Elizabeth's belief in the man she loved—and without her taking the time and care to sit him down and communicate that belief to him—things could easily have spiraled the other way and been devastating instead of uplifting.

Self-esteem can be as delicate as a flower. As every parent knows, a child's sense of self can be shattered by the taunts of a schoolyard bully or the unkind whispers of someone who was supposed to be a friend. That vulnerable child is still alive and well inside each one of us. Our own confidence is subjected to the buffeting winds of the world around us, and it can be a very unkind world at times.

Yet no schoolyard bully, no angry boss or carping coworker, has more power to undermine our self-esteem than our partner does.

Just as criticism is the opposite of appreciation, the destructive opposite of belief is contempt.

The *New Oxford American Dictionary* defines *contempt* as "the feeling that a person is beneath consideration, worthless, or deserving scorn." Contempt is not simply being critical of someone; contempt is dismissing the person altogether as having no value. This often shows up as a pattern of shame and blame or moral superiority, which can be lethal for a marriage.

It's normal to argue and even snap at each other. (In fact, the complete absence of all friction can be a sign of denial and bottled-up resentments; a surprisingly large number of divorcing couples say, "But we never fought!") Every couple has their own style of handling these situations. Often this is something we learned from our family of origin, and let's face it, all families have their patterns of dysfunction that do not always provide the healthiest model. It's important to learn how to disagree or quarrel without letting it escalate to an unhealthy place.

When your partner gets irritable, when they're tired or under stress, the key is not to take it personally; take a breath, stay level and supportive, and let their irritation be theirs. Be allowing. Even if they don't show it at the time, chances are good they'll notice and appreciate your calm response. They may even come back later and apologize for being so grumpy, and this can be an opportunity to talk about what's really bothering them and offer your belief and support.

Again, the key is to never let it get personal. Avoid escalating into an ad hominem attack. You might be irritated about something the other person *did*, but you never want to condemn them for *who they are*.

It's wise, for example, to avoid generalizations when you argue, such as the words *always* and *never*.

We were shopping together in a grocery store one day and overheard a man berating his wife. "You *always* do that!" he said. We have no idea what it was he was accusing her of *always* doing, but we've never forgotten the look on her face. He had, for all practical purposes, told her she was a terrible, worthless person because of this thing she *always* did.

He wasn't simply criticizing her *action*; he was negating her as a *person*.

Your Daily Practice

Take one opportunity each day to show or express your faith in your partner.

As with all the secrets, there are two parts to this process: first, cultivating a deep and abiding belief in your partner, and second, letting that belief show in your words and actions.

It's not enough to *have* unshakable faith in your partner. You also need to *tell them so*. And not just once, or now and then, but consistently. Why? Because sometimes we need to hear it over and over before we start to believe it ourselves.

Here is an example from our own lives.

John has been doing some form of writing all his adult life; for years it was editing other people's magazine articles, then writing his own articles, then editing and ghost-writing other people's books, and eventually cowriting books (like the original *Go-Giver*, cowritten with Bob Burg), all in the realm of nonfiction.

What he loved to read was novels, especially great mysteries and crime novels. But that wasn't what he wrote.

From the first time we met, I (Ana speaking here) believed there was a great novelist inside him. I started telling him that. "I think you would write *amazing* novels." He would smile and say he appreciated the vote of confidence—but then gently brush it off. He didn't believe it.

I kept reminding him—not constantly, not to the point of being obnoxious about it, just now and then. When he would tell me about some fantastic novel he'd just read, I'd say, "You could do that, too. In fact, I think it's what you were born to do."

He couldn't quite see it, but I could.

Fast-forward twenty years. The same year we wrote this book, his first novel was published to wide acclaim. (It's a thriller called *Steel Fear*, which he wrote with former Navy SEAL Brandon Webb.) Here's what John put at the opening of the book as his dedication:

For Ana, who always believed; for two decades you've been telling me I should write novels, until I finally believed it too.

Consistently sharing your unshakable belief in your partner over time builds a deep bank of mutual trust and confidence. It's a simple thing, yet as with all the 5 Secrets, putting it into practice every day reaps strong rewards. Everyone needs somebody to believe in them. *Everyone.*

Examples of Belief

While appreciation and attention may focus on a thousand little things about your partner, belief goes straight to the very core of who they are; it is your relationship's bedrock. You might express to your partner your belief in:

- their goodness as a person.
- their kindness and empathy.
- their integrity.
- their talent at (fill in the blank).
- their skill at (fill in the blank).
- their ability to (fill in the blank).
- their ambitions, aspirations, and life goals.
- what a phenomenal mother or father they are.
- what a great friend they are.
- what a great husband, wife, or partner they are.

Grow

Every day, identify what you need to be happy,
healthy, and fulfilled—and then give yourself that.
Dare to dream a bigger dream for yourself.

Why It Works

Every one of us is on a journey to become the person we've always dreamed of being. That journey begins in infancy, as we establish our core sense of who we are, and then grows through childhood and young adulthood, as we learn to integrate our own existence into the context of relationships and communities. One of the central challenges in marriage is the ongoing balance between these two: maintaining our own sense of self while also accommodating the feelings, experiences, needs, and wants of another.

In our love and admiration for our partner, we often want to join or merge in ways that seem innocent and healthy but that ultimately may undercut both our own individuality and theirs. This can also lead us to take on roles where both partners are supporting one person's dream, rather than each pursuing their own individual dreams and goals within the context of a supportive partnership.

Marriage is the ultimate test of individuation. Can we be a fully committed couple and at the same time exist as two separate, evolving adults?

One of the most common misconceptions about marriage is that the marriage itself is going to make us happier. That life with our partner is going to fulfill us in ways we don't feel adequate to fulfill ourselves. This fallacy can lead to disappointment, unhappiness, and resentment that undermine the marriage and sabotage its chances for lasting love.

The key here is to remember who we are as individuals. As Sofia says, "Marriage is a tree—and you are the soil. If the soil is exhausted and depleted, then nothing can help the marriage. You want to heal a marriage? Feed the soil."

Individuation is one of the hallmarks of a healthy marriage: you both get to be individuals, with your own interests and needs that don't compete. Marriage isn't meant to be something that swallows us up; it's meant to be something that supports, nourishes, and reinforces both marriage partners.

As Jeremiah tells Tom, "The purpose of marriage is to give yourself to another—and in the process, become your best self."

In a way, the first four secrets are about the front half of that sentence, and the Fifth Secret is about the latter half.

What It Looks Like

As Jeremiah says in the story, the 5 Secrets are all based on the core idea of giving—putting your focus on your partner's needs, wants, and happiness. Appreciating *them*, attending to *them*, allowing *them*, believing in *them*.

However, this does not mean denying yourself or sacrificing your own growth and happiness "for the good of the family." If you are a parent, you are modeling for your children what it means to be an adult. Do you want to embody someone who is open to continuous learning and new adventures—or someone whose development has ground to a halt?

The opposite of growth is stagnation. Letting yourself stagnate by denying or suppressing your own growth as a human being not only hurts you; ultimately, it also hurts those around you.

In fact, you owe it to your partner to grow. Building a healthy, long-lasting marriage means bringing your best self to that marriage. The Fifth Secret is all about the practice of finding and creating that best self.

There is a fantastic line in the film *As Good as It Gets*, when Jack Nicholson's character, who struggles with OCD and a host of other psychological challenges, tells Helen Hunt's character that because of her, he has started taking steps to manage his symptoms.

"You make me want to be a better man," he says.

That is a powerful expression of genuine love: *I love you so much that I want to be my best self.*

Let's revisit the case of Sarah and James from the Third Secret, *allowing*, as their story also provides an excellent example of *growing*.

Once James realized that he was trying to control Sarah's behavior in order to manage his own anxiety, he became more supportive and compassionate.

Sarah not only felt tremendous relief but also realized how much she wanted to work on her post-traumatic stress (PTS) responses and heal her anxiety. She didn't just want to be understood and attended to. She wanted to *grow*.

She began working with an EEG neurofeedback practitioner, using this modern therapeutic technology to retrain her brain's automatic response to challenging situations. She also committed to making time each day for a forty-five-minute meditation, designed to calm her through deep breathing and guided imagery.

In addition to the neurofeedback therapy and meditation, Sarah spent the next three years exploring the creative process as a healing path for recovering from PTS. She studied the subject with several renowned teachers. In the spring of her third year, she began offering creative therapy groups to women seeking drug-free approaches to healing anxiety. She brought in artists, dancers and movement therapists, and a variety of healers to teach and speak to her group, and she produced several guided-meditation CDs.

As an outgrowth of healing herself, she moved on to teaching and writing about healing anxiety and helped others heal, too.

James, meanwhile, had always been interested in the topic of creative reinvention. As he gained further insight into his process with Sarah, he began looking for a way to pick the brains of thought leaders from around the world. After a year of research, he launched a podcast devoted to interviewing artists, writers, musicians, teachers, speakers, chefs, and people from all walks of life on what drove their creative process and how they nurtured their creativity.

Within a year, purely through word of mouth, James's podcast became quite popular.

In the years that followed, Sarah and James studied cooking together with a famous chef, took surfing lessons with another guest from the podcast, and studied a variety of other creative topics, all with his podcast guests.

Sarah and James both loved watching each other's new avocations unfold. They reported that not only were they happier and more fulfilled as individuals, but they also came to see each other as more interesting and multifaceted people.

Sometimes the greatest growth comes out of the most painful, difficult situations.

This was the case with Charles and Ingrid upon the birth of their first child.

Little Milo suffered an injury at birth that soon proved to have devastating repercussions. His reflexes were impaired; he had difficulty feeding. Within weeks the young couple found themselves numb with grief and helplessness, a stark and painful contrast to the joy they'd been expecting to feel.

The pain and devastation caused by challenges like Milo's have enormous implications for the parents' ability to stay on course as a couple while also attending to their child's intimidating array of needs. As their pediatric neurologist quietly pointed out, the divorce rate among parents of special-needs children is 85 to 90 percent. "Try to stay on the same team," he urged them. "Don't let your grief and frustration get the best of you."

Easier said than done. The first few years of parenthood were a roller coaster of emotion as they learned to navigate their new situation. Gone were the normal milestones that most parents revel in—baby's first words, baby's first rollover, baby's first crawl. Instead they dealt with an endless parade of therapists, specialists, feeding problems, and developmental delays. Like Tess in the story, Ingrid had to leave her job to care for their son when they realized normal day care was out of the question. It sometimes seemed like they had to take turns grieving the loss of the life they'd expected.

However, amid the stress of being thrust into the dual roles of parents and full-time developmental therapists, they fell deeply in love with their son.

Ingrid kept a journal, writing notes each night about Milo's needs and responses from that day. She documented the games she played to enable his early movement and made little picture books to help teach him to connect language and images.

She made friends with other parents of special-needs kids and learned from their shared experiences.

By the time Milo was ten years old, Ingrid had become a special-education specialist, though without degrees or formal training. She learned all the special-education laws of their state and became a powerful advocate for their child, both in and outside the classroom. In addition, she opened a coaching practice for other parents who needed help navigating the laws governing the public education process for children with special learning needs.

Charles got involved with a nonprofit that supports children with special abilities and within a few years became a regional director, advocating for inclusion for children with special abilities. He began telling their parenting story at a local speakers group; soon he began to speak and consult regularly about the unique challenges and joys of raising a child with special abilities. Eventually he went back to school and got an advanced degree that enabled him to teach and consult on a range of related legal and educational issues.

Through all of the struggle, growth, and learning, Charles and Ingrid also managed to stay on the same team. Even amid the perplexing, often frustrating whirlwind of raising Milo, they took care to appreciate each other, to look out for each other's needs and make space for each other's feelings, to continue being each other's safe harbor and believing both in their child and in each other. Perhaps most importantly, they stayed open to the blessing of the growth they were all experiencing.

Ten years after his difficult birth, Milo was thriving well beyond the specialists' expectations, and Ingrid and Charles were happier and stronger in their marriage than ever before.

In their words, they not only grew; they grew up.

Your Daily Practice

Spend at least one hour every day doing something that brings you closer to who you're seeking to become—to being your best self. Build your cathedral.

If the Fourth Secret is believing in your partner, the fifth is believing in yourself—and *doing* something about it!

This doesn't necessarily have to be something sweeping and dramatic, like Jeremiah taking off to climb the world's tallest mountains or Ingrid and Charles becoming experts in their new fields. Sometimes taking care of yourself in small ways makes a big difference.

Growing can be as basic as taking care of your health, fitness, and peace of mind; starting that yoga practice you've dreamed about; cleaning or organizing your space; arranging your environment in your home or office so that it provides the beauty, calm, inspiration, flair, or whatever other environmental qualities nourish you. It can extend to your clothes and personal appearance; it might mean moving bedtime forward a half hour so you get a little more sleep and are more rested.

But growing also means investing time and energy in pursuits that support you in becoming who you want to become. Taking a class. Joining Toastmasters International and developing your speaking ability. Or taking a photography class, maybe with the goal of creating professional-level work.

Is there something you have always wanted to do but never allowed yourself the time and resources to pursue—or never quite let yourself believe you could?

Perhaps, like Dee, you want to return to college to pursue a career that makes you feel whole. Or pursue an avocation that has always fascinated you. Learn to write, to paint, to dance; to teach or coach; to pilot a plane or become a beekeeper.

Learning new skills not only keeps you young and vibrant, but also keeps the love alive—because it keeps *you* alive and growing.

Examples of Growing

Your relationship is a foundation and springboard for you to become the fullest expression of yourself, the person you've always dreamed of being. Paths to help take you there might include:

- going back to school, whether to earn a degree or simply expand and deepen your knowledge.
- taking a painting, photography, or other creative arts class.
- writing that book, that poem, or that collection of memories you've always thought about writing.
- learning a martial art; learning a language; taking cooking classes.

- joining or starting a book club, cooking club, or other group of curious, like-minded people; making new friends based on shared interests and aspirations.
- launching a new career or avocation; moonlighting or volunteering in an area that has always interested you.
- traveling to new places, going on hikes, going camping or on other adventures.

Love Is a Verb

We've covered a lot of material here—but don't feel you need to remember it all or master every detail. The central point in all of the above is simply this:

Love is a verb.

It's not something that just happens and keeps happening on its own, forever and ever till death do you part. It's something you actively, consciously *do*, day in and day out. Love, in other words, is not a state of being.

Love is a practice.

The 5 Secrets are five ways not just of being in love, but of exercising and deepening that love.

Because *appreciate* is really just another word for love. In fact, all 5 Secrets are simply five faces of love. You could describe them this way:

- *Appreciating* someone is telling them what you love about them. "I love your smile. I love your courage. I love how kind you are."
- *Attending* is finding tangible ways to demonstrate that love. "Here, let me show you how I love you."

- *Allowing* is extending that love in times when it isn't as easy, when your partner is dealing with some kind of stress. "I love you even in the ways you're struggling—especially in the ways you're struggling."
- *Believing* in someone is seeing and loving that person's very essence. "I love the very core of who you are, no matter what."
- *Growing* is showing your love by becoming the best self you can be. "I love you enough to become my best self possible—because you believe in me, and because I love myself, too."

We wish you the very best—for you, for your life, and for your lasting love.

A Go-Giver Marriage
Discussion Guide

Many of our readers have explored the Go-Giver *books together in their book clubs and study groups or among friends and family. The questions below may be helpful in guiding your discussions of* The Go-Giver Marriage.

1. In chapter one, Jeremiah Janell is interviewing Tom for a position as COO of a large company. Yet instead of asking him about business or his current skills, he asks him, when he was a kid, what he wanted to be when he grew up, and what he wants to do when he retires. Why do you suppose he asks these questions? What is he getting at, and why?

2. In telling his fable, Jeremiah describes each secret as a "gift," and he says the first gift is appreciation. Have you ever had someone in your life—your spouse, a relative, teacher or coach, friend or coworker—who consistently appreciated you? If so, what impact did it have on you?

3. When Nicole says, "Love is not blind. Love has the eyes of an eagle" (chapter four), what do you think that means? Have you experienced this yourself?

4. When the young man brings the princess cinnamon tea and she rubs his aching shoulders (chapter five), Jeremiah describes this as "paying attention." What are some ways that you and your partner pay attention and attend to each other?

5. In chapter seven, Melanie tells Tess the Third Secret is to "allow." What does it mean to allow? Can you think of examples in your life of someone who was consistently allowing? What impact did that have on you? Are there examples where the opposite was true, when someone was *not* allowing? And what impact did *that* have? Why is allowing so important in a marriage?

6. Several times in the story, the tree in Jeremiah's fable suddenly exhibits new powers. It produces roses (chapter three), then a variety of flowers, a flurry of fruit, and a bursting of birds (chapter five). Finally, its leaves turn to gold and silver (chapter eight). What does the tree represent, and what is the source of these transformations?

7. In chapter seven, Melanie says the professor told her that the "four deadliest words in marriage" are "I love you, *but* . . ." What makes these four words so deadly, and why? Have you experienced any instances of "I love you, but . . ." in your current or past relationships? What impact did they have on you?

8. At the end of chapter seven, Tess suddenly decides to send Tom a text telling him what a great father he is. What prompts her to do this? When Tom reads the message in chapter eight, what impact does it have on him?

9. In chapter nine, Sofia tells Tess that she shut down her practice as a couples therapist early in her career and reopened it a year later as a marriage coach, working with just one person at a time. What do you think about the idea of working on your marriage by focusing on changing yourself and your approach to the relationship?

10. Sofia tells Tess that belief is the Fourth Secret and that when you "really fully believe in" someone you love, "miraculous things take root" (chapter nine). Have you ever had someone in your life who consistently, unwaveringly believed in you and told you so? What effect did this have on you?

11. In chapter ten, Jeremiah describes how in the young couple's fifth year there were no storms at all, just a pervasive freeze—and this was the year their little tree came the closest to death. What sort of situation in a marriage do you think this describes? Have you ever experienced a "long, silent freeze" like this in your relationship or observed it in the relationships of others you know?

12. At the end of chapter ten, Jeremiah finally answers the question he asked Tom back in chapter one: "What is the purpose of marriage?" Do you agree with his definition? Why, or why not? How would you define the purpose of marriage?

13. In chapter eleven, Dee tells Tess about what she calls the Pindar Principle: "The more you give, the more you have." Do you think this is true? Why, or why not? How

does it relate to marriage and relationships? Can you give examples from your own life that might illustrate this principle?

14. In explaining the Fifth Secret, Dee tells Tess, "It's not your job to make your husband happy. And it's not his job to make you happy. That's something we all need to do for ourselves" (chapter eleven). Do you agree? Why, or why not?

15. In chapter twelve, Jeremiah says that the sound of the leaves in the tree—its *susurrus*—is the leaves whispering "thank you" in ten thousand ways, in ten thousand voices. Earlier (chapter five) he describes it as the "language of love." What does this mean to you?

16. Whether you are married or not, which of the 5 Secrets— appreciate, attend, allow, believe, grow—resonates the most for you? Why? What does that secret mean to you, and how does it appear in your relationship?

17. Which of the 5 Secrets, if any, do you see as the biggest challenge for you? How so? What steps might you take to address that secret in your relationship?

18. Can you think of relationships in your life other than your marriage (for example, relationships with your children, parents, friends, or coworkers) in which you see yourself using any of the 5 Secrets, and what does that look like?

19. Were you surprised in chapter thirteen by the conclusion Tom came to about the position he'd been interviewing for? Do you think it was a good choice for the two of them? Why, or why not?

20. The story ends with Tess sitting next to Tom and saying, "Tell me more" (chapter fourteen). Why do you think the authors concluded the story this way? What does it say to you? If you were going to tell a parable of your own marriage, what would you write as the closing scene?

A Conversation with the Authors

One of the best things about the experience of writing and producing the Go-Giver *books is the dialogue we have with our growing sphere of readers. Here are some of the most frequent questions we've heard about* The Go-Giver Marriage, *along with our best efforts to answer them.*

What led you to write this book together?

AGM: We've been talking through the concepts in this book for more than fifteen years, ever since John and Bob Burg wrote the original *Go-Giver* and we saw how profoundly it touched people, not only in their businesses but also in their personal lives.

In my coaching work, I'd also seen how the therapy model for helping couples, valuable as it could be, was often impractical. Aside from being an additional expense, it also required that both people in the relationship be equally on board with the idea of working on their marriage. In many marriages, that simply isn't the case.

I became keenly interested in developing an approach that people could implement on their own that engaged them in everyday acts of generosity and would build the marriage in tangible ways.

JDM: We were both raised by parents who remained married their whole lives, for half a century or more, and we witnessed firsthand their commitment to talking things through, staying on each other's team, and consistently building each other up. All four of our parents were constant cheerleaders for their partners in all aspects of their lives, and their example had an enormous impact on both of us.

We also both knew the pain of divorce from our own experience—and now know what it's like to be profoundly happy in a long-term marriage, where each day feels like a safe and loving oasis from the rest of the world! We wanted to share what we've lived and what we know in a simple, practical format, just as we'd done with the other *Go-Giver* books.

Do both people in the couple need to practice these 5 Secrets for them to work?

AGM: Absolutely not. The best thing about the book's approach is that it's based on each person changing their own attitude and behavior in the marriage—even if that's only *one* person.

When you start working on yourself, making the 5 Secrets a daily practice in your marriage, that change alone can reap powerful rewards. Your spouse may not be engaged at first or even aware of what's happening, except that things just feel better. When you drop the scorecard and start consistently voicing your appreciation for your partner, they feel it. In fact, the whole family feels it. There's nothing quite like the warm glow that comes from being authentically witnessed.

What often happens is that one person initiates the process, but it soon starts catching fire with the other person, too.

And that's true of all the 5 Secrets: as one person begins to practice them, the other one feels the benefits, and often what started as resistance or reluctance turns to openness and even active participation.

In our experience, couples want their marriages to make it; sometimes they just get off track, falling into patterns of blame, stalled communication, and impasse.

Ana, what impact did your early work in marriage therapy have on the approach in this book?

AGM: Fresh out of graduate school, I trained and collaborated with a very skilled and renowned therapist who introduced me to the work of Dr. John Gottman. In the couples therapy groups we co-led, we taught couples to turn toward each other when challenges arose, rather than distancing from each other and becoming more isolated.

We also implemented many of Dr. Gottman's concepts (borne out of his many years of original research) about communication styles in marriage, such as teaching couples to calm down instead of letting disagreements escalate to the point of full-on fights, complete with criticism, contempt, and a host of other dysfunctional patterns.

Dr. Gottman's work, along with that of many other therapists, teachers, and coaches, has had a profound influence on my perspective on marriage and couples dynamics. *The Go-Giver Marriage* is also the culmination of many years of both failure and success in love that have guided my learning and growing, and for all of the above, I am deeply grateful.

It doesn't seem like Tom and Tess are having major problems in their marriage; it's not as if they're having terrible fights or are on the verge of divorce. Isn't their situation pretty mild, even benign, compared to that of most real-life couples with marital problems?

AGM: It's a great question. The mildness was actually intentional. We thought about opening the story with a much more dramatic conflict, but the truth is, a great many marital problems start out exactly this way: like the rumbles of distant thunder long before the storm arrives in full force. Couples often just drift apart, slowly but steadily.

In fact, a lot of couples who wind up in marriage counseling or divorce court say they didn't realize just how serious their issues were until something blew up that made it impossible to ignore. And practically speaking, it's a lot easier to heal a marriage in those earlier stages than later on, when the patterns have become ingrained and the conflict has reached critical mass.

What's one simple thing people can take away from your book that will make a difference in their marriage?

JDM: One is the idea of "throwing away the scorecard." Some have said it's almost like withdrawal, because it's so easy and so tempting to keep score. Yet when you keep score, you both lose. As Sofia says in *The Go-Giver Marriage*, "A fifty-fifty marriage is a formula for failure."

AGM: Another is that it's not your spouse's job to make you happy—that's actually *your* job. This is the Fifth Secret: *grow*.

There are so many ways to keep growing and learning while expanding and deepening one's sense of self.

Self-respect lies at the core of every other kind of respect. To build a whole marriage, you need to be or become a whole person yourself. Your relationship is going to be only as healthy as what you bring to it.

When you talk about putting your partner's needs first, are you talking about sacrificing your own happiness for another's?

AGM: We are definitely *not* talking about being self-sacrificing or self-denying. You don't grow lasting love by being a doormat or a martyr. It's a matter of making your partner's happiness your priority, not at the expense of your own happiness but as an essential part of it.

JDM: And remember this: when you pour your love and attention into another person, the benefits flow to you as much as to them.

That's the Pindar Principle: the more you give, the more you have.

I'm having a bit of a tough time with the idea of putting "unshakable trust" in another person. What if my partner has gambled away the mortgage money, or been unfaithful, or done something else that makes me feel I can't trust them?

AGM: You're right, those are genuinely difficult situations, and they may call for professional support. But there's an important distinction here: there's trusting a person's every action and behavior, and there's putting your trust in the core of who they are.

Everyone makes mistakes and suffers lapses in judgment. In a marriage, we're often called on to forgive each other our stumbles. If your spouse has a history of being terrible with money, it makes sense to agree that maybe you're the one best suited to handle the family finances. Some lapses are so grievous that they may fatally undermine your ability to trust your partner. And yet, many marriages have survived episodes, for example, of infidelity. It depends on the marriage and your partner's willingness to change and grow together.

What about people who came from dysfunctional families? How do they learn to be giving and other-focused when this wasn't modeled for them?

AGM: This is a profound question that gets to the root of a lot of marital problems. Every family has some form of dysfunction, whether it's issues with basic boundaries, fighting, alcohol, neglect, abuse, or even depression in either parent. Children absorb this stress like a sponge, which results in them not getting their primary needs met and instead developing adaptive responses for handling everyday life. Children who grow up with neglect or abuse don't naturally gain the skills that loving parents impart, and are forced instead to make up their own version of what being a "healthy adult" looks like. Once they are in an intimate partnership, the ability to maintain this façade of normal adult behavior easily falls apart, and the relationship starts to falter because they lack the skills to function at a healthier level.

In my work, I have been deeply influenced by the work of Alice Miller, Pia Mellody, and Terry Real. All three have expressed in great detail the pain and self-sabotage that abused and neglected children face as they try to mount a "normal" life with healthy relationships. Adults who survive abuse and neglect often have difficulty with parenting as well, because they never experienced healthy parents themselves. These same adults frequently experience depression (whether overt or covert) as a symptom of the stress that the effort to function in the adult world creates. All these factors contribute to the need for greater education and awareness of the ways that both childhood and adult trauma reverberate in our lives.

No matter what the roots of dysfunction are in a child's life, they will have an impact on the child's function as an adult. The first step toward growing beyond these patterns of dysfunction is to become aware of them and how they are harming our personal relationships—and then, to consciously choose different responses and ways of being in relationship to another person. These 5 Secrets are based on the foundations of early narcissism—the developmental stage of life that touches our deepest desire to be seen, witnessed, understood, and believed in. Many marriages have been saved because the individuals, like James in our chapter on "Allow," were brave enough to face the neglect and abuse from their childhood and create new patterns of behavior.

In the book you consistently talk about marriage; the word marriage is even in the title! Do these secrets apply only to

married people, or can they also be applied to people in a relationship who aren't married?

JDM: We believe there is something unique about marriage and its totality of commitment. Even though many marriages don't end up surviving for a lifetime, that is still generally the couple's intention at the outset.

At the same time, there are also plenty of couples who are not (or not yet) married per se, yet whose relationships are marriages for all practical intents and purposes.

AGM: And yes, the 5 Secrets can absolutely be just as helpful to couples who are dating or in a not-yet-long-term relationship. The main difference is that when a relationship is still on a "we'll see how it goes" basis, there may not be as much incentive or dedication to work things through to their ideal place. This is especially true of the later secrets: allow, believe, and grow.

Still, every relationship of any kind is a coming together of two people, and the same basic human needs apply.

Can I use the 5 Secrets in relationships and situations other than marriage?

AGM: Yes! While this book is focused on your marriage, you can also apply most of what you read here to your relationships with other people, including your children, coworkers, business partners, and friends.

Obviously, there are differences based on the nature of the particular relationship. Still, it's striking how much the same principles apply. Everyone thrives when they are appreciated. Everyone responds to meaningful gestures of personal attention.

Everyone needs space or a little extra support sometimes. And so on. Yes, it's about marriage—but fundamentally it's about honoring the core developmental needs we all share in common.

In the original *Go-Giver* you had "Five Laws of Stratospheric Success." In this one, you have "5 Secrets to Lasting Love." Is the recurring number five a coincidence, or are they connected somehow?

JDM: Definitely not a coincidence! Every one of the *Go-Giver* books is wrapped around a set of five principles. When we started taking a close look at what we wanted to say about different aspects of human interaction—leadership, influence, and now love—we saw in each case that it mapped very well onto that original set of five "laws."

If you take the Five Laws of Stratospheric Success from the original *Go-Giver* and put them next to the 5 Secrets to Lasting Love, you'll see some interesting correlations.

One key aspect of these "fives" is that the fifth principle always seems opposite or contrary to the first four, but it's actually the complementary principle that makes the first four work. It's like the way your fingers and opposing thumb work together: without a thumb it's awfully difficult to paint a picture, write a book, or build a cathedral.

There are quite a few characters in this story who seem like familiar faces from the other *Go-Giver* books. What was the idea behind that?

JDM: You're right. The three women Tess meets at Sofia's home all hail from earlier *Go-Giver* parables: Nicole from *The Go-Giver*, Gillian from *The Go-Giver Influencer*, and Melanie from *The Go-Giver Leader*. Our story takes place about fifteen years after the events of the original *Go-Giver*, so they've all aged accordingly, and Rachel's Famous Coffee, which had just gotten started at the end of *The Go-Giver*, has now become "a massive global enterprise."

AGM: We wanted Tess to interact with three women who'd all experienced very different challenges in their marriages. Nicole, like Tess herself, has had no dramatic breakdown, just the unsettling sense that her marital bond is gradually drifting apart. "Like a nagging cough," as she puts it, "that you sense could turn into something worse." Gillian has gone through a divorce and is on her second marriage; Melanie and her husband, Ben, have suffered through the loss of a child.

JDM: We also thought it would be fun for readers who knew the earlier books to see old friends turn up again! We haven't seen Pindar since the first book, though he's been hovering in the background throughout. We think of the city where all these stories take place as "Pindar's town."

Do I need to read the other *Go-Giver* books first, before I read this one?

JDM: Not at all. There are definitely elements from the earlier books that will make the reading of this one richer—you get to learn a good deal more about Pindar, for example, as well as the whole *Go-Giver* philosophy—but *The Go-Giver Marriage* is designed to work as a stand-alone book.

Once you've read it, we'd certainly recommend reading the other books, too. You'll find there's a lot in those that also applies to relationships in general. *Go-Givers Sell More*, for example, is really about a good deal more than sales, and *The Go-Giver Influencer* says as much about relationships as it does about how to be a person of influence.

If I want to read the other books, where should I start?

JDM: I'd begin with the original *Go-Giver*. That's where it all started! In fact, there's a chapter in that book, a scene between the main character, Joe, and his wife, Susan (it's chapter nine), that in many ways was the seed for this book.

As Pindar tells Joe the following day: "These lessons don't apply only to business, Joe. A genuinely sound business principle will apply anywhere in life—in your friendships, in your marriage, *anywhere*. That's the true bottom line. Not whether it simply improves your financial balance sheet, but whether it improves your *life's* balance sheet."

I notice that Bob Burg, your coauthor for all the other *Go-Giver* books, isn't listed as a coauthor on this one. Did he have anything to do with this book?

AGM: Bob is a huge part of this book! Although he's never been married himself (and thus didn't feel qualified to participate in the coauthorship—typical Bob humility), his parents, Mike and Myrna Burg, provided him with a powerful example of a stratospherically happy marriage when he was growing up. Even today they are a big part of his life, and the life lessons he learned from them have been a major influence on the philosophies behind all the *Go-Giver* books, including this one.

JDM: Even though Bob decided it wouldn't make sense for him to be a named coauthor, he's been close to the process and you can feel his influence on every page. The three of us—four, actually, including Bob's business partner, Kathy Tagenel—have been an inseparable working team on everything we've done in the *Go-Giver* world right from the start.

Any final words?

JDM: Yes, one more thing: *laugh.* I consider it one of my primary duties as a husband to make my wife laugh. Every day. A lot. If you ain't laughin', you ain't livin'.

AGM: My final thought is this: While we don't discuss intimacy directly in our little story, we definitely address it in our *Go-Giver Marriage* Coaches training program. Bottom line: keep your love alive in the bedroom. Practicing the 5 Secrets will deepen your love *and* the intimacy in your marriage. So keep laughing—and practice!

Acknowledgments

This entire *Go-Giver Marriage* project has been a labor of love right from the outset—not only for the two of us but also for a growing team of people who have devoted their time, skills, and dedication to making this book a lasting reality. Our thanks go out especially:

To Bob Burg and Kathy Tagenel, our partners in all things *Go-Giver*, for your pivotal role in turning our original little book into a worldwide movement of millions. We love you and your tireless dedication to bringing *Go-Giver* values to the world!

To Margret McBride and Faye Atchison, our literary agents, for believing in *The Go-Giver Marriage* way back when it was no more than a twinkle in our eye.

To Glenn Yeffeth, founder and publisher of BenBella Books, who caught the vision of this book in an instant and loved it from Day One; Leah Wilson, our editor in chief, and Rachel Phares, our dedicated in-house editor; Sarah Avinger, our excellent art director; Lindsay Marshall, our phenomenal marketing director; Adrienne Lang, our deputy publisher; Monica Lowry, our production director; Jennifer Greenstein, our intrepid copy editor; Sarah Beck, our outstanding endorsement wrangler; Alicia Kania, our vendor content manager; and everyone else at BenBella; we couldn't dream of a more perfect publishing partner.

To Gregory Brown, our brilliant editor and author of the beautiful novel *The Lowering Days*, for his delicate hand and keen insights in helping to bring our manuscript over the finish line.

To Adrian Zackheim, founder and publisher of Portfolio and godfather of the first four books in the *Go-Giver* series.

To Will Weisser, assistant godfather, who has been a pivotal part of the *Go-Giver* series for over a decade and offered us invaluable feedback and advice in the final stages of this manuscript.

To Randy Stelter, friend and educator, for taking the lead in bringing *The Go-Giver* to America's classrooms and for inspiring and coauthoring *A Teacher's Guide to The Go-Giver*.

To our circle of early readers for their insights, enthusiasm, and good will: Deb and Charlie Austin, Jimmy Callaway, Dan Clements, Donna DeGutis, Bill Ellis, Phil Gerbyshak, Rob Hawthorne, James Justice, Adrian Mann, Abbie McClung, Patricia Petty-Munns, Erin Neuhardt, Dan Rockwell, Tara Rogers-Ellis, Dondi Scumaci, Ken Smith, and John Stetler.

To Faye Atchison, Beverly Bellmore, Stephanie Braudrick-Gerbyshak, Bill Ellis, Andrea Gold, Kevin LeBlanc, Erin Neuhardt, and Tara Rogers-Ellis for their expertise and invaluable input on our cover design.

To Erin Neuhardt, for helping us navigate the world of podcasts and social media marketing.

To Dr. John Gottman, author of numerous bestselling books on marriage, for his pioneering work in marriage research and his ongoing efforts to educate people and help save their marriages.

To Terry Real, for opening the door to a deeper understanding of the hidden elements of depression in men and the inequity it creates in marriages around the world.

To Susan Cotter-Davis, M.A., Dr. Robert Emery, and Dr. Ruth Holt, for their wisdom, insight, and friendship in the earliest days of this journey.

To Neil Gaiman, for being the inspiration behind our "fable within a parable" about the young man, the princess, and the magic tree.

To Marguerite Crespillo, for being the inspiration for "Nicole's Story"; you can read about Marguerite's own story in her wonderful little book titled (of course) *100 Things I Love About You*.

To Maren Baldwin, Kate and Art Galyen, and Shawn and Robyn Ruggles, for helping our lives, household, and dog Phineas all run smoothly while we were writing this manuscript.

To the many marriage and relationship podcasts and radio shows that have graciously hosted us, asked deep questions, and helped to share the 5 Secrets with others, and especially Sharon Thiel at WARV-New England Life Changing Radio, for opening doors to many other national radio stations.

To our Go-Giver Marriage Coaches team: you are the light that changes marriages every day. Thank you for all that you do to make the world a more loving place, one relationship at a time.

And finally to you, faithful reader: here's to your lasting love—and to becoming your best self!

About the Authors

JOHN DAVID MANN is an award-winning author whose writing has earned the Nautilus Award, the Axiom Business Book Award (Gold Medal), and Taiwan's Golden Book Award for Innovation; *The Go-Giver* earned the 2017 Living Now Book Award's Evergreen Medal, given for the book's "contribution to positive global change." John's books are published in three dozen languages and have sold more than three million copies. In addition to coauthoring the bestselling *Go-Giver* series with Bob Burg, which has sold over one million copies in thirty languages, he is also coauthor of the *New York Times* bestsellers *The Latte Factor* (with David Bach), *The Red Circle* (with Brandon Webb), *Flash Foresight* (with Daniel Burrus), and *The Answer* (with John Assaraf and Murray Smith), and the national bestsellers *Out of the Maze* (with Spencer Johnson), *Among Heroes* (with Brandon Webb), *The Slight Edge* (with Jeff Olson) and *Real Leadership* (with John Addison). His *Take the Lead* (with Betsy Myers) was named Best Leadership Book of 2011 by Tom Peters and the *Washington Post*. His first novel, *Steel Fear* (coauthored by Brandon Webb), was released in 2021 and hailed by Lee Child as "sensationally good—an instant classic, maybe an instant legend." John is married to Ana Gabriel Mann and considers himself the luckiest mann in the world.

ANA GABRIEL MANN, M.A., holds a master's degree in clinical psychology and dance-movement therapy from Antioch New England, where she specialized in working with adults and family therapy. She went on to train and work with renowned Israeli-born therapist Dr. Ruth Holt, a marriage and family specialist who taught couples to identify their patterns of dysfunction and cultivate "love maps" based on Dr. John Gottman's landmark research. Together they led a highly successful series of therapy groups that gave couples a window into the dynamics of the other marriages in the room. Following her work with Holt, Ana served as clinical director for a New England–based program providing county-wide therapy, education, and services for family members caring for individuals with Alzheimer's disease; and as adjunct faculty and student trainer for Antioch New England, utilizing movement therapy to draw on long-term memory in individuals with Alzheimer's disease to facilitate emotional connection and wholeness. In 1984 she cofounded the New England Institute for Integrative Acupressure, New England's first college of Chinese medicine, where she co-led programs through 1997. For the past two decades she has worked primarily as a corporate consultant, speaker, trainer, and business coach in both profit and nonprofit sectors. In addition to coaching and teaching the 5 Secrets to Lasting Love, she is the creator and lead facilitator of the Go-Giver Marriage Coaches training program.

The Go-Giver Marriage Coaches Program
Are you a personal coach or thinking of becoming one?

John and Ana 's **Go-Giver Marriage Coaches** training and certification program will train you in the art of coaching and mentoring individuals who want to improve their marriages.

As a certified Go-Giver Marriage Coach, you will be licensed and trained to teach the *5 Secrets to Lasting Love*™ and help individuals bring these skills to life in their own relationships. You will also learn the essentials of how to establish your business as a Go-Giver Marriage Coach. As part of the program, you will:

- Gain a deeper understanding of marital dynamics while learning the coaching skills you need to facilitate positive change for your client base.
- Work directly and individually with Ana Gabriel Mann and senior GGM coaches in the supervised application of the curriculum in your own practice.
- Learn how to set up your own Go-Giver Marriage Coaching practice, or add the *5 Secrets* skill set to your existing coaching, counseling, or mentoring practice.

Designed for individuals, coaches, clergy, mentors, and all who seek to help build a world of lasting love, this program provides a complete curriculum of instruction, ongoing supervision, and listing in our Go-Giver Marriage Coaches directory.

gogivermarriage.com/programs

Don't miss these other titles in the bestselling *Go-Giver* series!

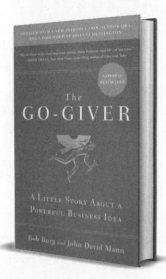

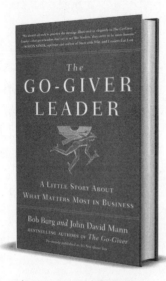

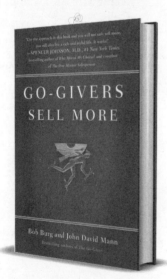

Wherever books are sold. Or visit
gogivermarriage.com/books